Nurturing
Business Leaders

Zero-based Proactive Learning Paradigm

Nurturing Business Leaders

Zero-based Proactive Learning Paradigm

Dr. Saumya Sindhwani (India)
Dr. Theresa Loo (China)
José Guillermo Alejandri Rodríguez (Mexico)

Foreword by
Prof. Gary Davies
Manchester Business School, UK

STERLING PUBLISHERS PRIVATE LIMITED

STERLING PUBLISHERS PRIVATE LIMITED
A-59, Okhla Industrial Area, Phase-II, New Delhi-110020.
Tel: 26387070, 26386209; Fax: 91-11-26383788
E-mail: mail@sterlingpublishers.com
www.sterlingpublishers.com

Nurturing Business Leaders
© 2009, Sterling Publishers Pvt. Ltd.
ISBN 978 81 207 4593 3

All rights are reserved. No part of this publication may be reproduced, stored in a retrieval system or transmitted, in any form or by any means, mechanical, photocopying, recording or otherwise, without prior written permission of the publisher.

PRINTED IN INDIA

Printed and Published by Sterling Publishers Pvt. Ltd., New Delhi-110020.

Dedicated with our love

to

our parents

&

also from

Saumya to her

aunty Adarsh and uncle Ranvir Trehan

Foreword

At the time of writing this foreword to *Nurturing Business Leaders: Zero-based proactive learning paradigm* the commercial world is in crisis. A collapse of the banking system may or may not have been averted by an unprecedented intervention by almost every government in the developed world. Billions of dollars of public money have been pumped into a financial sector that has, perversely, provided one of the main sources of employment for the most highly qualified and highly paid in our society — the best trained strategists from our top business schools, those relatively well equipped to forecast the future and devise strategies to ensure that their businesses could adapt to at least the obvious challenges in the environment. They have failed and their failure has been spectacular.

The most common metaphor being used to describe what has happened is that of a tsunami, a tidal wave of such proportions that it is capable of engulfing and destroying all that stands in its way. I prefer the metaphor of an earthquake because solid buildings can survive a tsunami and provide refuge for the humans sheltering inside them. Only an earthquake can destroy the foundations of apparently solid buildings, bringing what seemed so secure moments earlier, crashing down, taking with it most of the wealth of the humans lucky enough to survive. I would argue again that while a tsunami cannot be predicted and cannot always be detected in time to protect a society, earthquakes can be predicted with some certainty. Lending mortgages well above the value put on a property by realtors or estate agents, in other words commission-based sales people, to high-risk customers in a market that has a history of cycles in price, does seem to be a flawed strategy. Unless one is clever enough to bundle that debt up with less risky lending and sell it using derivatives of the original loans, which conveniently makes it less than transparent what that parcel of debt really contains, until the music suddenly stops and whoever is holding the parcel finds that inside it is a worthless piece of paper. Then it becomes a winning strategy for whichever genius constructed the package and the derivative that wraps it and disguises it. But it is a winning strategy only until the investors whose money you are ultimately lending start to lose confidence in your ability to repay and prefer to put their money literally under their mattresses. Lenders are the foundation of the financial system. If they disappear, the system collapses. So why didn't we see this coming? Why were bankers allowed to lend 120 percent of the value of a house in one country whereas in another there were saner rules limiting lending to 70 percent?

This failure of management is unfortunately not the first to be laid at the door of the business school sector. The corruption that was Enron and those banks, accountants and investment analysts associated with its genesis, flowering and eventual collapse, have also been associated with the large number of MBAs from leading business schools employed (particularly by Enron) and the teaching of the 'new' business model that the company represented in those same business schools.

The less than fragrant demise of this and similar symbols of modern day capitalism has led to a reappraisal of the assessment process for business schools used by at least one validating body. Ethics and social responsibility, once excluded from the curriculum, are the latest buzz words to dominate faculty boards and appointment advertisements. Maybe this is shutting the stable door after the horse has long gone, but ethical issues are also at the heart of the banking collapse and will be at the heart of the next crisis. Bankers are still in denial. This was not their fault. They point to the regulators and their inability to understand the complexity of derivatives and other financial instruments that created an industry of mathematically-driven decision making, one bereft of common sense. They point to the active encouragement of governments in promoting their financial sectors and a willingness to turn a conveniently blind eye towards the increasingly obvious excesses of the banking sector. The media point, with the benefit of 20/20 hindsight, to what they now claim as an increasingly worrying level of dependency of economies on a mushrooming financial services sector. For sure the bankers are to blame for their greed and their inability to manage greed. But let us not forget that the math behind much of modern banking was developed in the University and Business School sector. Some of the mud has to stick there too.

I remember one of the classes I attended as a student myself nearly 40 years ago. It was about week six and the subject was accounting and finance. One student, who always sat at the back and with an impatience that suggested he already knew most of what the lecturer had to impart, suddenly exploded. "When," he shouted, "are you going to tell us how to fiddle the books?" We all laughed thinking this was a great if rather ill-timed joke. The only funny thing about it was of course that it was not meant as a joke. The student was serious. So are business schools, and is business education about, in some ways at least, teaching students how to break the rules but not get caught? That appears to be the paradigm that some students expect of us. For sure, finding smarter ways of making money faster could be one description of a business education.

What is so ironic about the bailout of the banks by governments, particularly those of America and Britain, is that what has had to happen is akin to nationalisation, in other words socialism — anathema to the free-market philosophy of even the New Labour party of Tony Blair and Gordon Brown in the UK and most certainly to the Republican president of the USA, George Bush. As the cast of the tragedy — that has been modern capitalism — exit the world stage hanging their heads, enter stage left an actor carrying a new model of business, China. Is China a communist country, is it a developing country; what is it? For sure the standard of living of its citizens, while relatively low compared to that in the West, is more likely to be growing while you are reading this book than that of the country I live in. Is theirs then the business model that I should teach next term to my MBA class in strategy?

This leads me neatly into talking more specifically about this book and its content. We need more ideas, and ideas that are more radical, if only to be better able to see our existing models of business in perspective. The three authors are each young Turks, products of the business school system and now working in different economies from those where they studied. Their book provides a good starting point for further discussions about designing a new pedagogy for business schools around the world but also for any business person trying to look into a crystal ball as to what might rise from the ashes of recent months. It should also provide those, with responsibility for management development in employers around the world with ideas on the skill sets and thinking they might need to develop in their existing management cadre. The book is well crafted from a series of interviews with the good and the great of business but it contains much original thinking too from the authors. You won't agree with all of it, but it will stimulate your thinking and by doing so, help improve the education of the next generation of would-be tycoons.

November 2008 **Gary Davies**
Manchester Business School

Preface

Tomorrow is uncharted. How does one step into uncharted territory? Unprecedented change mandates extraordinary change. Change to manage the changing change. How is change changing? What is its intensity or its direction? How is it different from the past trends? Do we require different management processes, knowledge bases, skill sets, managerial mindsets and management education systems for the evolving knowledge era? Do we require different leadership processes and mindsets?

What does globalisation really mean? What is new about it? What does globalisation globalise? How? Is it manageable? How? Is it possible to give it a direction? Is it desirable to give it a direction? Does globalisation augment localisation? What are the local-global dynamics? What new business paradigms do we require to remain competitive and sustainable in the evolving knowledge era?

What is so new about the knowledge era? Some say, multidimensional disruptive change is the hallmark of the information and knowledge era. What kind of innovative management thinking and practices do we require to meet the challenges of the fast-evolving new era of instant global connectivity and networking? What would be the new challenges for managers and business leaders in the evolving global business arena? How different will tomorrow be from today? What forces will shape the future business and social models as well as their relationships in the evolving social-cultural-economic milieu? How will the strategies, structures and business processes of business corporations differ from those of today?

What traits would be essential for future change managers and business leaders? How to nurture future learning leaders? Perhaps, leaders with deep local insights, global values, social consciousness and global perspective; performance-focused inspirational leaders who are transparent and can glue their teams with trust, yet take nothing for granted. Assume nothing. Question everything.

These and many more such questions form the basis of this book.

People have their own perception of happenings around them. Informal and unstructured queries at different interaction points provided us the general thinking of people at different vantage points. The perceptions highlighted the problems, challenges, threats and opportunities in the evolving scenarios. Our aim was to learn, gain insights of happenings and, if possible, find an alternate way forward. Our efforts were to bridge the gap between the what-and-how of the education system and the what-and-how requirements of the real corporate situations. Or what would be required of management students as corporate players? What pedagogy would be more effective? How would the business players be evaluated in their career?

The new era has brought with it various disruptive technologies and accelerated changes — instant global connectivity, new business process options and new context. Thus, we felt the need for a zero-based proactive learning paradigm. Proactive learning ability would be the greatest asset for individuals, corporations, as well as nations in the evolving era. Recent failures of big business players with hundreds of star MBAs from best business schools in the world clearly demonstrate the need for a zero-based approach to reconstruct our management education.

We feel, besides other features, our paradigm provides a holistic integration of proactive, participatory enquiry, project and live problem-based learning. It may also be seen as a synthesis of learning, teaching, consultancy and research.

Preface

When we discussed the proposed paradigm with some experts, we were encouraged by their response. A large majority of them said it was simple, usable and transformational. Proactive learning is and will be a critical success factor in the fast-emerging knowledge era. For the new era we need to think anew.

We are not sure when our curiosities and informal interactive learning venture morphed into a hazy structured manuscript — a milestone in our learning venture. As far as we can remember it all started as a fuzzy enquiry over a cup of green tea at the Quad in the London School of Economics and Political Science with a business development manager of a USA-based business consultancy firm visiting London. The idea was to get an overview of the world of management and perceptions of globalisation. Later, less nebulous and somewhat focused inquiries, often with our doctoral research guide at the Manchester Business School cafeteria, encouraged us to continue with our learning venture.

The backdrop to the queries kept changing. Starting with Saumya as a masters degree student at LSE, the inquires continued during our doctorate degree programmes as well as post-doctoral assignment at the Manchester Business School of one and the teaching assignments at the Leeds University of the other. From UK the scenario shifted to India, China, Mexico and to various other global locations. Also from academics it often extended to different streams of the world of global commerce and geo-politics. Thus the readers will experience a lot of gear shifting, in topics and perspectives.

Our inquiries were learning focused — inquiries expressing our desire to understand the present and get glimpses of the way ahead. Most of the meetings were unplanned, often unexpected and usually impromptu. Almost, each informal interface with a business player generated a situation, profession and industry-based interaction. Also, the discussions often continued over extended transnational conversations, SMS messages, chats and emails.

As stated above, this book is an outcome of our unstructured and informal self-learning exercise. It is an assemblage of perspectives of different people from different walks of life, at different times, in different countries, at different universities, colleges and B-schools, and at different places such as airports, during various flights, seminars, tea breaks, emails, chats and informal gatherings. The interactions were more often casual, informal, unplanned, intuitive, situation specific, spontaneous and frequently reflective in nature. It is an effort to understand thinking and perceptions of different sets of people about the future and on different aspects of management, globalisation, localisation, management education, strategic perspectives, new business model options and talent development alternatives.

We strongly feel that the paradigm suggested will develop managers and business leaders who understand change intuitively and see it as an exciting game and are not afraid of it. It would make management and leadership learning more interesting. Also, the zero-based questioning-learning centric paradigm is inclusive as it helps in developing students, faculty and research as well as consultancy activities of B-schools.

In a way, this book is a compilation of learning interactions of the authors in different parts of the world and an extended effort to share their learning and thinking.

At the outset, we must confess that this book suffers from many limitations. It is just an effort of three students of management, located in three different countries, who were lucky to have a once-in-a-lifetime opportunity to have the same wonderful guru in the fourth country in one of the leading and the largest universities of the world.

The book may be seen as a small compilation of random global perspectives. It provides, among others, perspectives of a number of CEOs, opinion leaders, social workers and business players on the current state of management and management education. The book may also be seen as a summary of their shared thoughts on the happenings around them, their concerns and desire for a better future.

We make no claim of presenting a representative point of view of any group. The book provides some shifting kaleidoscopic views without any scientific sampling or pattern. Nor do we claim of any discovery of any realities about the mysteries of management processes or the increasingly complex world of business. It may also be seen as a vignette of informed individual thoughts on management and management education in the global context. Also, originating from different parts of the world in different languages, our translation efforts may have made some observations and concepts fuzzy. We apologise for our shortcomings.

We are very grateful to all those who took time to respond to our questions and spared time to explain their views in detail. We tried not to get emotional about the issues discussed. However, at times the dialogue did get emotional, harshly honest, brutally frank and animated. We are not sure how far we have been successful in presenting the views the way each one may have liked. We apologise for our failures. Due to various reasons, many of the people we interacted with did not want to be identified. To maintain harmony and honour our commitment to them, none of the respondents have been identified by name or nationality.

Our enquiry started with our attempts to understand the prevailing concepts of management and globalisation. The interactions and responses created the desire to gain insights of the global business arena and the emerging challenges as well as opportunities. Perceptions and discussions on these topics generated curiosity to know the thinking of the global business players about the alternate response options as perceived by them and their vision of future business models and job profiles.

As mentioned above, our inputs are mainly based on unstructured interactions, chats, emails and some correspondence. As expected, an unstructured approach brought in many diversions, digressions, surprises and emotions. At times readers may feel there are repetitions; there are some and we apologise for that. But as we moved around we found people had the same concerns. Often the same or similar points were explained by different people differently, in different languages and in different contexts. At times we had to amalgamate similar views expressed in different languages. Thus the book provides jottings of unstructured, informal, often emotional and open interactions.

It is often said that appropriate education is the key to sustainable economic development. But, what is appropriate? We still don't know. In a very limited way this is an exploration in that direction. Our overall focus was to gain glimpses of the future and understand the concepts of management, gain some insights of the issues involved in global business operations, talent development and management education.

As we tried to gain an understanding of the business world during our discussions with people from different industries, it became apparent that there were many gaps between existing talent development methods and the expectations of corporations from their independent human resource developers, such as business schools. In this book we have tried to present an alternative approach to developing future managers for social, economic and business organisations.

Keeping in view the dynamics of business scenario as well as inputs and information available to us, we feel convinced that it is time for rote teaching to give way to proactive learning for future managers. Management, we believe is the most creative of the creative activities and should be taught creatively as well as innovatively.

Preface xvii

Introduction of management concepts and leadership challenges at an appropriate time and in an appropriate way, we feel, would go a long way in developing enthusiastic and effective managers as well as leaders for each area of human activity.

Given the vast global information base, mobile and continuous connectivity, the onus of learning must rest with the future managers. To stay in competition, learning would have to be proactive as well as continuous and lifelong.

The global talent hunt emerged as the common underlying theme of most discussions. This culminated into the evolution of alternate ways for developing future need-focused talent. Based on our learnings, we have ventured to suggest an alternative approach to management education and inculcation of leadership traits with social insights. It is a presentation of our thinking. It is not an attempt to prove or disprove any theory or hypothesis. We would feel amply rewarded if our efforts are able to make even small contributions in enhancing effectiveness of management education in developing more insightful business leaders and proactive entrepreneurs.

We are grateful to our respective organisations for giving us the opportunity to learn and share our learning. However, the views expressed by the authors are their personal and do not reflect the thinking of the organisations with which they are individually associated.

A very vast number of business executives and business school faculty members from various countries and different industries have contributed to the development of this book. We would like to thank each and every one of them. We hope, among those who read the book will be able to read their own words and hear their own sounds. The idea of structuring inputs into a book evolved much later.

We would like to make special acknowledgements of a few who helped us in giving the project its direction and destination. The book is a milestone in our learning from various formal and informal interactions in different parts of the world. Some have a special role in it.

At LSE, Saumya often discussed the concepts with her classmates while walking from one class to another or during chit-chats over cups of tea and coffee. Also many very useful insights on the various topics were provided by late Prof. Claudio Chiborra, Prof. Shirin Madon and Prof. Steve Smithson.

Manchester Business School provided various opportunities to the three authors for long discussions over cups of coffee, lunch, dinner and during long walks through the city. Our colleagues from different parts of the world provided us diverse and insightful perspectives on globalisation as well as business processes. In-depth understanding of various concepts was provided by Prof. John Murphy, Prof. Paul Jackson and Prof. Naresh Pandit.

Whenever at the crossroads, Saumya would rush back to Prof. Kamlesh Misra and Prof. Umashankar Venkatesh, her mentors from college days for direction and the way forward. Uncle, Dr. Jayanta Madhab, also an LSE alumnus, with his warm smiles and hearty laughter, was a constant source of encouragement and learning explorations for her.

Last and most profoundly we, Saumya and Theresa, want to take this opportunity to express our thanks to Prof. Gary Davies — our guru, guide and friend. Guillermo wishes to convey his special thanks to Prof. Francis Chittenden. Most importantly we thank our parents for their full support and encouragement in pursuance of our learning enquires.

Saumya individually wishes to express her personal grateful thanks to her aunty Adarsh Trehan and uncle Ranvir Trehan for their unconditional support, guidance and encouragement in pursuing her academic ventures and career path. Words fail to express my heartfelt sentiments and feelings of gratitude. Thanks a million aunty Adarsh and uncle Ranvir. Saumya also thanks Manoj Vohra for his constant encouragement and support. Thanks Manoj.

The three authors individually and collectively express their very warm and grateful thanks to their parents and humbly dedicate this book to them and Saumya's aunty Adarsh and uncle Ranvir Trehan, residing in the USA.

We are very grateful to Shri S. K. Ghai, Chairman and Managing Director of Sterling Publishers for his guidance in transforming our unstructured notes and the draft manuscript into a reader-friendly book. We would also like to express our heartfelt gratitude to Sonia for editing our work and making it reader friendly and for her patience in managing three authors sitting in different parts of the world.

We are aware of our limitations and know we have lots and lots to learn. We need to experiment with our concepts and develop more appropriate learning tools and formats for the same.

We would be very grateful to our readers for their feedback to help us to ask more, see more, hear more, observe more and learn more as we move on with our experimental learning odyssey.

It has been a new learning experience for us all as the learning span currently covers India, China and Mexico in English, Chinese and Spanish to start with. Depending on the response, later we would like to incorporate other languages as well.

Dr. Saumya Sindhwani
Dr. Theresa Loo
Mr. José Guillermo Alejandri Rodríguez

Contents

Foreword vii

Preface xi

1. Management Musings 1
2. Globalisation Perspectives 26
3. The Global Business Arena 45
4. Challenges and Opportunities 60
5. Response Options 74
6. Emerging Global Business Models and Job Profiles 89
7. The Global Talent Hunt 115
8. Nurturing Proactive Business Performers 127
9. Developing Young Intuitive Managers 166
10. Future Challenges and a Way Forward 181

1

Management Musings

"Management is God, or you may say, God is management." This is how a senior vice-president of a transnational corporation in the telecommunication industry responded when asked his perception or definition of management. He went on to elaborate, "Tell me an activity where there is no management? Things and environment are constantly changing around us. Change is life and life is all around us. Each change is an experiment in life, living and management. All are being managed. It may be good management or bad management but management is here, there, everywhere in the universe. It has always been there, it will always be there. Knowingly or unknowingly, we are all managers, managing our available resources with our given abilities, to attain our objectives. For me, 'we' includes all the birds, animals and the plants; the total world of flora and fauna."

With a candid smile on his face, he got up from his executive chair and walked towards the large office window. Looking out, he invited us to join him. Pointing towards a tree outside he said, "You see that beautiful nest there. You can also see the bird. I have been observing that bird for the past few weeks, almost from the time she had zeroed in and decided to make her nest there. Do you think it would be possible to make a nest like that without planning, organising, proactive self-leadership and control? Exactly those very principles of management and strategic management which my father sent me to learn in USA. I wonder, how much designing, structural engineering, decision making and time management would have gone into making that nest. For the safety of her offspring, she would have taken into account security and hazards study as well. She has predators hovering around her all the time. Show me a management concept that is taught in B-schools that has not been used by her. I am not talking of the skills of finance, information technology or marketing. Frankly, with all my technical and management experience as well as a very prestigious MBA degree from one of the best B-schools in the world, I do not think I would have the common sense to select that site for nurturing my kids; or design that nest with the limited resources as are at her disposal. I feel humbled by her."

After a little thoughtful pause he continued, "How different is it, from the management perspective of a large corporation searching for a location for its production unit? In fact, I am in the same management process right now. I can empathise with that bird. Only I feel inferior, considering the complexity of her operations in selecting the site and creating a site-specific intricate creative nest, especially in view of her limited resources. I call her Migi (my inspirational guru ji). I feel I have a lot to learn from her."

He stood there looking out silently as if meditating, offering silent salutations to Migi. After a while he said, "I don't know if I am making any sense to you or not. Encouraged by your patient listening and open-ended approach, I wanted to share some of my silly little thoughts on management with you."

As we shook hands to leave his office, he concluded with a smile, "Management, I feel, is not a human monopoly. Management is nothing if not creative. Frankly, I feel it is the most creative of the creative arts. If we look around, management genius, management splendour and management stupidities are all around us." We parted with a warm handshake and a thoughtful contemplative silence.

Elaborating on the topic, the lady CEO of a large traditional jewellery manufacturing and export organisation said, "I feel every religious book, I would not like to name any scripture for fear of hurting sentiments of any one sect as well as our own *Vedas* and *Upanishadas*, are a treatise on management — management of self and society."

Moving on with her explanations she said, "After all, at the end of the day, management is the art and science of resource management. Nature manages its resources, birds and animals manage their resources and we humans are learning to manage our internal and external resources as individuals, as family units, as corporations and also as national economic units. For me resources include our emotions, personal energies and our ability to focus. Frankly, we are not doing a very good job of it. We have a lot to learn from nature and the day-to-day activities around us."

After a short pause she elaborated, "We are all managers from the time we come on this earth. Even a newborn baby manages herself, her physical and entertainment needs. She also knows how to get work done from others around her," she said with an indulgent smile of a young mother.

Elaborating on the perception of management, a senior business executive in the advertising industry said, "Management is a power game. Knowingly or unknowingly, each manager creates his or her own brand power." He went on to elaborate, "All religions are branded services. We have a lot to learn from them about branding and management. Each sect has created its own brand equity. Individuals, leaders, kings and nations have been creating their own brand equities since prehistoric times. Brands have been used to consolidate social, economic and nowadays corporate power."

Another business player in the information technology consultancy organisation explained his observation on management in these words, "I am not a student of history but I believe, that like the successful products and services of today, religions must have experimented with their services. There must have been many failures as well as adaptations and re-formulation of their compositions and service-mix offerings on the way. Even nowadays I find several successful religions and spiritual leaders have adapted to their market or clientele needs. Intuitively or from feedbacks or even from competition, they must have learned to understand the expectations of their followers. They have created their own sophisticated brands. I feel we can learn a lot from their experiences especially in the areas of customer relationship management (CRM) and customer interface management (CIM), which are an integral part of business management."

Elaborating on the above theme, a senior professor of an institute of technology said, "Most studies in science are efforts to understand nature's principles of management. Be it in the areas of physics, chemistry, medicine, psychology, astronomy or nuclear technology, we are only trying to learn how nature manages its operations. We are only at the initial stages of learning. Management is an integral part of systems around us. We are only trying to de-code it and understand it."

Elaborating on similar lines, the head of a spiritual organisation said, "Management is an integral part of nature. Management creates. Management preserves. Management destroys. It is not a result of any system. It is not an outcome or a creation of any economic or political system. It is *Brahma*. It is *Vishnu*. It is *Mahesh*. It is a continuous holistic process in nature around us."

After some elaborations he concluded, "Management takes us from one cycle to the next. It can take us from one level to the other. It all depends on our own abilities to master it. Master our internal systems as well as our external relations."

A retired army general said, "Management is the art and science of reaching targets with minimal loss or optimal use of resources." He went on to elaborate, "To achieve success, one must critically evaluate one's own capabilities, acquire as much knowledge about the area of operation as one can, identify the target, understand the nature of competition and competitors and evaluate each available alternative before initiating a move. I think in the current business context it is called strategic domain knowledge."

We received the above and the following responses because of our unstructured and open-ended approach to understanding concepts of management of people in the different walks of life and in different segments of society. Majority of them happened to be executives from different industries.

We interacted with people from different parts of the world, in fact, whoever we could; through emails, face-to-face interactions with participants during tea and lunch breaks in various international seminars, over the phone and internet chats. A good number of people we interacted with had received MBAs from globally well-known business schools.

A senior vice-president of a Fortune 500 Corporation articulated his views thus, "The future culture of the world will be a management culture. Different countries and societies will have different hues of it. However, the core of it all will be management."

After elaborating on the above observations, he went on to explain, "Globally we are increasingly operating in an environment of rising expectations in every area of human endeavour; be it economic, social or political. Resources are limited. Disparity is increasing. Consumer and citizen activism is on the rise. For social harmony, we will need to find sustainable managerial solutions. We will need to improve governance of our social institutions. We need to critically examine the efficiencies and cost of management of different social, political and corporate activities. Each of these has its own dynamics, targets, priorities, resource constraints and management style."

He went on to elaborate, "India has a population of over one billion, about one sixth of mankind. As we know we have very low levels of social amenities. If we are to raise per capita standards of consumption in basic items such as intake of food, consumption of cloth and provide minimal levels of housing — *roti, kapra aur makaan* — what is the magnitude of resources and management acumen we require? Just to enhance per capita consumption of cloth by one meter per person, we would need more than one billion meters of cloth over and above our present production. Try and picture the resources, related talents and investments we require to produce, store and distribute that kind of output. Similarly think about the possibilities of upgrading consumption of food and housing on per-capita basis. Frankly I cannot even comprehend the problem."

"How much and the variety of management talent will we require in future? I really don't know," he said thoughtfully, after a long pause.

"Today, management should be a concern of everybody. In fact, I feel everyone should be trained as a manager. We need more effective managers in social work, rural and urban activities, politics, education, culture and every other field. We live in a competitive environment. Tacit and explicit competition between individuals, families, communities, corporations and nations is increasing every day. We all have to be aware of our opportunities and responsibilities to make ourselves, our families, our community, our organisations and our country more competitive," said a lady entrepreneur, CEO of a fairly large printing organisation.

She went on to elaborate, "We should take an integrated view of management. Management is not an exclusive business or corporate activity. It is practiced in government, judiciary, politics, social institutions and families as well. Basic principles of management remain the same in all these operations."

After some discussions she went on to say, "Today many of the transnational corporations are larger economic units than some nations. If there is an age limit for retirement of CEOs of transnational corporations then, it seems logical that there should be an age limit for politicians also. After all, just like CEOs they get paid for designing and managing national policies."

She further went on to observe, "Even when there is change all around us, at times I feel we are surrounded by too many old and archaic ideas, status quoism and obsession for obsolete because these have become emotionally comforting clichés."

Another lady entrepreneur from the publishing industry observed, "Why do we make such hue and cry about management, as if it is a new discovery. Business schools are in the race for inventing new management jargons. Human history is full of individual, national and global management achievements. Take a look at the historical monuments and achievements around the world. In our own case, Kautilya (300 BC) demonstrated the art of identifying and developing leaders as well as creating and managing a large empire, perhaps the largest of its time, without the help of modern day information technology. His *Arthshastra* is a management treatise. His elaborations on situation specific use of strategies and his suggestions that the weak may be controlled by *sama* [conciliation] and *dana* [placating with gifts], and the strong by *bheda* [sowing dissension] and *danda* [force] are even valid today. And, if you want to study strategic management, analyse the thinking and operational activities of Krishna in the Mahabharata war. In more recent times, Mahatma Gandhi provides us many examples of value-based strategic thinking. I believe management principles are the same. Only we need to master their situation-based applications. This is what players do in games also."

"Management is a game of common sense. Not even uncommon common sense, just simple common sense. It is a game of proactive learning, clearly-defined objectives, smart thinking and determination. Most entrepreneurs in India and abroad have proved it," she summed up.

Founder of a large NGO observed, "Societies are living systems or organisms. So are corporations — living organisms and sub-sets of societies in which they operate. Thus, instead of taking a micro or specialised view of management like in business, finance or marketing, we should also try and take a holistic view of management. Nations and now the whole world is becoming an integrated human and economic entity. There are many organisations such as the United Nations, World Bank and the World Trade Organisation that need to take a global management perspective. Many business corporations are larger economic entities than national units. We need a new global approach to management. A more integrated approach that covers individuals, families, organisations, societies and nations. Management is universal in nature. Today, it has a common global language and many common global concerns. "

He went on to elaborate, "Management that we normally talk about or read in the papers is a very limited and narrow perspective of management, mainly concerning business units and usually limited to a few skilled-based activities such as finance, marketing, production and co-ordination of human resources or talent management. Within each activity, jobs are further classified as low-level, middle-level or high-level management and as strategic or non-strategic. Each corporation has its own caste structure and each activity its own sub-caste system."

After a short pause he went on to elaborate with a smile, "Frankly I feel, I may be wrong but I have my constitutional right to be wrong. All activities are a dynamic mix of managerial fundamentals. Many routine, which may be termed as low-level management activities, are an integral part of a CEO's day-to-day agenda. Also, many so called low-level managerial activities are critical success factors for every organisation. Management, instead of focusing on performance in resource management, has evolved into a corporate caste system. Business schools have their own caste system. At times I can feel vibrations of a very rigid caste system, which often gets reflected in organisations and international business meetings."

Elaborating on the above lines a chief economist of a mutual fund said, "Self-interest is the prime mover of capitalism. Value or profit generation are direct measures of ones virtue in the corporate world. Each individual tries to highlight his contribution or virtues. Management jargons, like recitation of Sanskrit *mantras*, are used to reinforce ones position. Frankly, I feel, there has been, and there will always be a caste system in every human society. It may be based on the power of knowledge, nature of economic activity performed, or acquisition of power or a brand equity generated by any other means. Justified or not, the business school caste system is also based on one or more of these."

Giving his perspectives on management another senior economist, associated with the banking industry said, "Perhaps management activities should be demarcated and discussed on the lines of the three clearly demarcated commercial activities namely, transactional activities, transformational industrial and agricultural production activities and tacit operations which require higher and often abstract levels of personal judgements. I feel management in each of these — social, economic and political activities require distinctly different levels of knowledge bases, skill sets and mindsets or attitudes." He went on to explain,

"Value chain economics as well as attitude, skills and knowledge required for transactional activities is vastly different from those required in transformational and tacit knowledge-oriented activities. I feel all these need to be examined and studied comprehensively and distinctly for all social, economical and political activities around us."

After some elaborations, he went on to conclude, "Critical success factors for managers and leaders are different in transactional, transformational and tacit operational activity zones, be it in social, economic or political domains. Also, success and failures are defined differently in each domain, at different times in different situations."

A senior national administrative services officer observed, "I think your reference to management and management education is in the context of management as practiced in corporations, large and small and in their day-to-day business operations. It is a very recent and young study of a management sub-set. The business education as taught in business schools is only about a hundred years old. Also, as I have observed, and I can only say it with my own limited experience in some leading business schools, it is more business-skills oriented rather than management-process oriented. Management in general is a very complex activity. It is much more complex and multivariable than visualised by business schools. In the curriculum of B-schools, management is generally a low priority subject. Also, very few B-schools offer specialisations in management. Some leading B-schools talk of leadership as their unique selling proposition (USP), but leadership without strong fundamentals in management, may be just rhetoric, or possibly a prescription for failure, as I see it. I may be wrong. But to me it sounds hollow rhetoric without substance."

After elaborating on his observations he went on to say, "Think of management operations such as management of national economic systems, managing national growth, national governance, international relations management and social governance on a national and international scale. Corporations as we know them today are a relatively recent phenomenon. On the other hand management process is as old as mankind. Also, individually, corporations are a subset of a society, often with only one objective and limited accountability to a small set of stakeholders. That perhaps may be the reason for narrowly focused and skills-oriented approach of B-schools, as far as the subject of management is concerned."

After substantiating his statements with some examples he went on to elaborate, "No doubt corporations are prime movers in society, also a very critical part of society, but we need to keep things in appropriate perspective. Business school graduates should be aware of their limited domain knowledge and operational base. Because, I feel, B-schools teach them skills and not substance; rhetoric or jargons and not real contents. B-school graduates often present themselves with an arrogant know-all attitude."

After some elaborations he continued, "For example, challenges for a business manager, trained to sell products or services supported by high-priced consultants, advertising campaigns and supply chain management experts, for a profit, or manage finance operations by doing a limited set of activities, are very different from a manager in charge of a rural education and training centre for challenged people. The latter usually has limited resources, low remuneration and a much higher social responsibility and accountability. Here what is common between the two managers is their aim to make optimal use of available resources. This aspect is usually ignored by business schools. Business schools examine optimality of limited financial resources, by measuring limited financial results, for a limited period of time by providing limited products or services to a limited set of customers. All or most of their choice is a very limited micro-approach, I feel. Business schools need to grow out of their cocoons."

After some further elaborations he went on to say, "I seem to have generalised my limited observations, but I hope you get the point I am trying to make. Keeping in view the recent trends in technology — especially information technology, globalisation and increased competition for resources, we need to take a zero-based approach to management. In view of the evolving geo-political, geo-resource, geo-talent and geo-economic competition where efficiency of every national activity matters, we need to take a holistic view of management. I feel every citizen should think of himself and herself as a national manager with rights to define his or her own managerial functions and responsibilities. From the national perspective, I fail to see, how a person who manages maintenance or cleanliness of public roads is a less important manager than the one who manages or pushes the sale of shampoo or junk food with heavy advertising support? They are both managers, managing their assigned activities, operating within given parameters. Shouldn't both be part of the national management development system? I am aware that there are hard and soft sides of management, however, I feel every traffic jam, every accident and every delay reduces our national competitiveness. I feel our VIPs and ministers when they cause traffic jams, cause national wastage and hurt our national competitiveness. We need to be aware and improve every phase of our national management activity. We need to train every citizen as a national manager, with national resource concerns."

After a short pause he said, "We are all managers from the time we come on this earth. We practice management in our own ways and in our own management style. Life, after all, is a chain of decisions. Every job, in every phase of life, is a self-portrait of the person who does it. We need to autograph our work, whatever it may be, with excellence, to the best of our ability we are capable of. I feel that is what management is all about."

After elaborating on some of the points he concluded with the statement, "A good manager has to create a whole — a whole that is more than the sum of its parts. As managers we must make sure that we make positive contributions to whatever we do."

"I feel management is a game of general awareness and common sense. Of course, it is well known that common sense is not so common. Even before the MBA era started, human beings created wonders of the world. Many massive and complex projects were conceptualised, designed and implemented with rudimentary technologies. I really do not know what is so special about management studies or MBA. I know the MBA degree is expensive. How useful it is, I have no idea. Business schools benefit from students, but do the students benefit from their B-schools? My own experience with MBAs has been disappointing. I wonder whether any reliable cost-benefit study has been done to find out whether MBAs create or destroy wealth. Or, during the past 50 years who has created more wealth, MBAs or non-MBAs? There have been substantial corporate failures with MBAs on the helm. On the other hand gigantic industrial empires have been created by non-MBAs. At times, I feel management education or MBA curriculum is a commodity — a common structured framework for all B-schools, all countries and for all seasons. I am not trying to be cynical. I know you are an MBA. My son is also an MBA from a very famous business school in the USA. I would not like to make any value judgement on B-schools. I am just curious," said an entrepreneur CMD of an engineering organisation.

After some discussions on different aspects of evolving business environment, he went on to say, "One often hears of business schools teaching their students to be business leaders and provide out-of-the-box thinking, but my experience has been different. My experience has been that they are usually opinionated and have preconceived old case study or textbook based set responses to business issues, which is often very detrimental for business."

Expressing views on connected perspective, a senior lady executive from an engineering and consultancy organisation said, "Why such a big difference in cost and corporate acceptance between full-time MBA and MBA by correspondence or e-learning? Frankly I have discussed this topic at many forums, even with directors of some leading B-schools as well as senior human resource managers but have never been able to get a logical or even a satisfactory answer. The most common response I got was 'the value is in classroom discussions.' But, close-door classroom historical case study discussions between whom, in what time frame and with what insights? Each subject is assigned 20 to 30 hours of classroom time with about 60 students in each class. Also, usually the discussions take place between a few students and faculty, ironically most of them may have never worked in corporations or implemented a social project."

After elaborating on some of her observations she went on to say, "Correspondence and e-learning by executives are done while they are operating in real-business situations and interacting with other business players. Having been a high-fees paying, full-time MBA student in one of the leading B-schools myself, and also having attended some management development programmes conducted by faculty members who have never experienced agony and ecstasy of being a manager, I am unable to appreciate their responses. It is a well-known fact that most B-school faculty members have little or no industry experience. I have often wondered that during the two years of about thousand-classroom-hour MBA programmes, how many meaningful questions are raised by students. Frankly I can only recall a few; in fact, very few during my MBA days. Most business schools keep repeating the same or similar cases and textbooks. Years on, faculty continue to provide the same answers and similar solutions to even different case studies. I have often wondered, is it fair or ethical for B-school teachers who have never experienced business, to write textbooks for business students and teach them year after year. At times I feel B-schools float around in an isolated make-belief environment. Nothing seems to change in B-schools, even while they teach subjects such as creativity, innovation, entrepreneurship, leadership, change management and business environment dynamics."

After elaborating on some of her observations, she concluded with a smile, "I am sorry to sound so cynical. But, I feel, I do have the right to hold on to my views till proven wrong."

Speaking on similar lines a senior executive of an insurance company said, "Having been a student of a leading B-school and also a visiting faculty at some highly reputed business schools, I get a feeling that the institutes are locked in their own-created webs of 4Ps, 5 Forces, Six Sigma, 7Ss and some other pet business perceptions of dogs and cash cows. Also, by standardising pedagogies of courses and repeating few well-known case studies with almost set responses as well as similar pedagogies, they seem to be further commoditising their products and entrenching themselves in rote teaching mode or at least are in search of ways to standardise management education. The 'new' is in new jargons, not in substance. I feel it is a risk-enhancing mindset in a fast-changing business environment." After some elaborations he went on to say, "Based on my recruitment visits to various well-known institutes, I can say that the differences in the unique selling propositions (USP) of B-schools are mainly cosmetic and jargon based."

Another senior executive with an MBA from a world leading B-school observed, "Faculty in B-schools know they will be evaluated by students — their customers. Hence the customers' satisfaction is a critical success factor for their career growth. Faculty evaluation criteria are also common in most B-schools. Case studies provide a very effective win-win solution. After discussing one or two case studies in class we can pre-empt who will take what stand. It provides good entertainment, certainly more entertainment than learning."

After some elaborations he went on to say, "Like the most common mistake for batsmen in cricket, one of the most common reasons for failure in business is when managers try to repeat their successful formula. I often feel this is one of the major shortcomings in learning through case studies. Management, to be effective must be situation, context and people specific. Even faculty members often recommend similar analyses, techniques and solutions for different case studies. However, case studies make one feel so intellectual and logical in class. Class discussions on various high-profile global case studies seem so informative and entertaining and give the participants a 'virtual-global-CEO-halo' and a very pleasant 'feel-good-know-all' feeling. No one is concerned about the relevance or realities. One learns to be politically correct. Data, information and knowledge are accepted as synonyms."

After giving some interesting details of his faculty and classroom experiences in the world famous B-school, he went on to say, "Let us be honest and face realities; one does not go to the best ranked B-schools in the world to learn something extra. The extra is in the global networking opportunities, developing future business potentials with alumni and the exclusive well-recognised brand equity. That is what we pay for in the form of high fees and in return that is what corporations pay us for, as high remunerations. Frankly, I find many of my juniors are much less paid because they do not have a high global-brand MBA like me but are much brighter and better performers than me in the business game. But I am the *Brahmin* of the team, because of my high-profile MBA," he concluded with a smile.

"I wonder how frank I should be. With your international experience I think you will understand and appreciate my observations. Business schools, more so Indian business schools, teach management skills. Finance, marketing, information technology, production, even human resource management are taught as skill-defined ways of doing things. These are the core subjects of specialisations in most B-schools. B-schools are mostly skill schools, not management appreciation or management understanding schools. Finance, marketing, information technology and even human resource management are taught as systems and skills. Pardon my language, but that kind of teaching would only produce do-as-told management clerks, management coolies or at best subservient managers. Not competitive proactive learners and improvement or productivity-focused managers," said an expat lady country head of a MNC in India.

After discussing some of her experiences in different parts of the world, she went on to say, "I often wonder how much 'Indian' are the Indian managers? How much 'Indian' are Indian B-schools? Take a critical look at their course materials. When I travel around India with some of my Indian colleagues, who have been educated in the best of Indian schools, I am appalled by their ignorance of India, their lack of general knowledge and their own national cross-cultural insensitivities. Time and again, they are total strangers in their own country. I have also often observed that they are at a great loss, even when dealing with the opposite gender of their own country and at total loss when dealing with formally dressed lady executives of other countries. They often make a poor sight at business formal and informal group interactions. Some do not even know how to attend to their potential business partners, initiate informal conversations, shake hands or make eye contact, especially with persons of the opposite gender. Besides business etiquettes, I feel B-schools should also educate their students about the communication significance of postures and body language in public places. All these are critical in cross-cultural human interactions in establishing credible management networks. I feel Indian managers should try to become good well-informed Indian business managers before they aspire to be effective global business players. There is so much diversity around them and so many cross-cultural learning opportunities for Indian managers. They must learn to learn from the learning opportunities round them. Business is a game of commonsense. Look around, India is full of entrepreneurs. Streets are full of them. The police have a hard time clearing them off the roads. Ironically, instead of removing animals, the police remove wealth and employment-creating small and budding entrepreneurs from the roads. I feel that business reading, learning and reality should go hand in hand."

After sharing some of her interesting cross-cultural experiences in different parts of the world she went on to say, "Cultural sensitivities are critical. Let me share an example with you. We had prepared a well-researched sales pitch for an important project for a country in the Middle East. Near the end of the presentation there was a graph with a star to highlight the growth trends. Inadvertent use of stars created a major cross-cultural problem for us. We almost lost our chances to win the project." She went on to say, "I am often invited as guest speaker at many B-schools. I tend to judge the students and faculty by the nature of their questions. I feel the quality of questions reflect the level of learning or level of concern in a particular subject. There are times when students and faculty have nothing to ask any individual speaker or the panel and that can be really embarrassing — both for the school and the speaker; and it speaks out loud for the B-school," she concluded with a smile.

"I completed my MBA in the sixties. There was a shortage of business teachers and I was a reasonably good student so I was offered a teaching assignment in the same B-school. While teaching, I also gained my doctorate. I will shortly be retiring from my full-time assignment. I have taught at some leading B-schools in India and abroad. Frankly, I feel core subjects or pedagogy have not changed much in the B-schools during this period — few decades — almost half a century. Sure, some new subjects in information technology and other topics have been added in the curriculum and some technology has been introduced in the classrooms. By and large, I feel, there has been very little change in the thinking of B-schools. Personally, I often feel, I have also just changed sides in the classroom, from sitting on the student's seat to standing on the teacher's side," said a senior professor of a leading B-school.

After some discussions he went on to say, "Also, I sometimes feel that B-schools are trapped or locked in their self-created and fortified rote systems. Change is a common topic of discussion. Some well-known senior faculty members often ask, what could have changed or should have changed in management or B-school teaching? Why? From the teaching perspective, core business activities are still the same. Based on felt need, new topics and new editions of textbooks have been introduced. Industry continues to value B-school graduates, pays them well. MBA continues to be one of the most respected qualifications today. Faculty is paid well and also gets some consultancy assignments from industry. Students get to study well-structured programmes. With time and based on their performance, some B-schools have acquired brand equity. I have also written one textbook which I have been using in my class for more than a decade."

In support of his assertions, he narrated an interesting observation, "There is a well-known university with a reputed B-school, in North America. It is situated in beautiful surroundings on a hilltop. There was, maybe it is still the same, only one long road leading to it; to symbolically represent that there is only one way to learning. There were two basement floors for parking, administration, stores, etc. The two main floors were on pillars. Thus the pillars on the ground level separated the two floors, architecturally demarcating and separating learning from the mundane administrative activities. On the first floor there were classrooms and on the second there were faculty offices. The noticeable thing about the university architecture was that the beautiful outside view was blocked off from the classrooms. On enquiry, I was told that the architecture was based on the philosophy that education should be pursued in isolation from surroundings. Considering our own *ashram*-based learning approach, I feel that the prevailing method of teaching in B-schools may not be wrong."

After sharing some teaching and consultancy experiences he went on to say, "Like many other areas of social life, there have been many critical write-ups about B-schools as well. But as far as I know, no one has come up with any workable alternative or an alternative that would be more acceptable to industry or students. After all, marketing is marketing, is marketing; is it not? Same applies to finance, IT or HRM. B-schools learn from industry and each other. We have national and international academia-industry interactive conferences on different subjects. Frankly, I feel B-schools are doing a good job. Case study method introduces students to business realities. Textbooks give them a good base in business theories. This is what all B-schools are doing around the world. I have taught in some business schools in other countries also. It is a well-proven and a well-established method of teaching business subjects. In a democratic environment there will always be some dissenting voices. Overall things are all right, as far as I can see. However, I will be happy to know if here is a more effective or better way to teach business subjects in the given time frame. Frankly, I see no alternative."

The human resource vice-president of a MNC said, "Business schools have been teaching the same subjects in the same way over the years while the world of business has gone through a sea change. Over the past few decades the speed of change from an agricultural-based economy to an industrial economy and to the current service, information, and knowledge economy with new technologies and global connectivity, has increased manifold. Many new business models have come up. Business requires a new set of skills, domain knowledge and attitudes."

After giving details of some of the problems faced by him he went on to say, "When we recruit candidates from B-schools, mostly from well-known B-schools, we have to provide extensive training on our end before we consider them 'job-fit'. The B-school caste system does create corporate team building problems, at times. We have to put them through lots of unlearning and relearning. Diplomatically introduce them to some harsh ground realities of business; help them do a self-analysis of their strengths and weaknesses vis-à-vis the job for which they have been selected. Frankly very few B-school graduates know the job profiles they are looking for or they are fit for. One of the most painful observation that one comes across is that even after doing an MBA, most students do not know the profile of jobs they would really enjoy doing. The youthful enthusiasm is mostly missing. They often lack aspiration and the spirit of adventure for jobs for which they are selected and even for the undefined jobs they think they desire. They usually have a fuzzy idea of the industry they would like to work in."

After giving some examples he went on to say, "Corporations are complex dynamic living organisms. But, in business schools they talk of business activities in segments — marketing, finance, information technology, production, etc. It is like the discussion of joints, elbows, eyes, nose, without talking of the body as a whole or even the skeleton. It generates images like the perceptions generated by the six blind men when they experienced the different parts of an elephant's body."

After discussing some of the specific cases he went on to say, "Based on my experience, I would say that some of the weaknesses of B-school graduates include their lack of soft skills, including communication skills. They lack curiosity and the desire to learn. They hardly ever ask questions but are full of pre-determined answers. They graduate from B-schools with a know-all mindset. One-size-fits-all approach of B-schools develops many misfits. I feel the criteria on which B-schools are ranked are also faulty. As we often say in business, one gets what one measures. On an average, it takes us about two years of mentoring before MBAs break-even and become productive enough to cover their cost-to-the-company (CTC)."

Another vice-president of human resource management of a large multinational manufacturing and marketing organisation observed, "We have an elaborate filtering process. We put the candidates from various B-schools through different tests to evaluate their suitability for our organisation. Once selected, the candidates are put through an even more rigorous training schedule, most often in different departments, to give them the kind of exposure they would require to take up challenging assignments."

After some observations she went on to say, "Our business schools give a very tainted and hyped up view of the business operations. They emphasise the glitter and glamour but underplay the competitive real hard work and harsh realities of the business world. I feel, B-schools need to spend time on defining professional profiles of their graduates. What are they expected or supposed to know? On joining the organisation, many new recruits are disillusioned and some even go through mild depressions. Recruiting and placing candidates is a time consuming and high-cost activity. Effectively replacing B-school images of the business world with factual ones requires emotional sensitivities also."

The country manager of an MNC stated, "Every organisation has a level of competencies. New recruitment is judged against that. We expect new entrants to help us move to higher levels of competencies; add value to our existing teams. Personally what I look for are team players with an enthusiastic open learning mind and commitment to learning as well as sincerity of purpose; not so much for marketing or finance skills. What I try to avoid are people who are ready with set textbook answers or have a touch of arrogance with a know-it-all attitude."

After discussing some of his experiences he went on to say, "Based on my own experience in B-schools and having visited some other B-schools, as well as having interacted with MBA graduates from different institutes, I feel here are some negative outcomes from our current management education system. Students seem to lose curiosity and enthusiasm to enjoy business as an adventure." After some elaborations he went on to say, "At times, I feel there is a major disconnect between B-school curriculum and pedagogy and the current corporate talent needs."

"I have mixed feelings about the MBA or PGDBM qualifications. Students also experience a divide between the expectations at the time of joining a B-school and at the time of graduation. Frankly, in my case, at the end there is a sense of disappointment. The hype and the expiations that are created by schools are really not well founded. The placement data is often misleading. The variations between the highest and lowest job offers — in quality, quantities and remunerations are seldom stated. Why such a big difference between students of the same batch is not explained. If inputs are quality controlled, why such a big difference in outputs? There are no correlations between B-school class performances and job offers. Placement efforts are student-alumni led, with minimal, more often indifferent, support from B-school administration. Jobs on offer are very different from our expected jobs. Placement is the key selling point of B-schools and main attraction for us also," said a student in the final term of his B-school graduation.

After some discussions on his experiences he went on to say, "The learning workload, such as required classroom attendance, lectures, assignments, presentations, internal exams, is so high in the school that one hardly gets time to discuss and digest the concepts. Frankly we did not even get time to read business journals; libraries are usually empty. Most of the time was spent in classrooms and the hostel room. One-to-one discussions with faculty members were seldom possible. Generally speaking, except for heavier workload, the life in B-school was not much different from the life during first degree university graduation."

"I feel it all depends on what one wants from the B-school. Many of us are here because MBA is the in-thing to do. It is the best degree option on offer at the moment. We will find our way as we move along," said a new entrant of a leading B-school.

"Frankly I feel we need to separate B-schools with limited objectives from our discussions on management. Parameter commonly used to evaluate and rank B-schools, include infrastructure, intellectual capital, reputation, admissions criterion, placements, industry interface and governance. The definitions of criteria are often fuzzy and usually there is no mention of the evaluation of the education process itself. Like any other process, the education process should be evaluated on the basis of difference between the inputs and outputs. The process may have positive as well as negative value addition. To rank educational institutions, some publications use a formula-based perception score. Here the parameters commonly used, include prevailing reputation of the institute, infrastructure, curriculum, quality of academic inputs, student care, admissions procedure and job prospects. The input-output ratio is again missing. Also, perceptions without clear definitions can be misleading. Criteria such as ethics, creativity, innovation, research, social responsibility, transparency and governance are usually missing from the evaluation criteria. The performance score card is neither balanced nor comprehensive," said a retired director of a leading B-school.

After some discussions on the commercial value and use of ranking by educational institutions he went on to say, "I feel we are really not serious about the objectives of education or about the critical role of management in our daily life or for improvement in the utility of resources available to us. Just look at the degree of wastage around us. For optimal results micro and macromanagement units should be in harmony."

"Keeping in view all the happenings in the global corporate world — where best-rated corporations by best-known credit rating companies go bankrupt overnight; where CEOs and senior executives award themselves with big performance bonuses while begging for public money to support their business operations; where banks, auditors, regulators and corporations loaded with high-profile MBAs refuse to take moral responsibility for commercial failures and extensive social sufferings — what is one to say about globally glamorous B-schools and the management education system? I feel the whole economic and corporate system seems to be in need of an honest zero-based analysis," said a senior bank executive.

As expected, different people have different perceptions of management and management education. A large number of respondents felt that management like other games is a competitive game of acquired knowledge, inherent capabilities and developed competitive competencies. For some, a game of institution, gut feelings, instincts and strategic mindset.

The above interactions provided us interesting learning opportunities in the range and expressed concerns of different respondents. It gave us some motivating perspectives on management and management education, an encouraging beginning; and also provided us a direction to move on.

2

Globalisation Perspectives

"Change, more change and still more change; competition, more competition and still more competition; that is what globalisation is all about," said a lady senior executive in the fashion export business.

After some elaborations on some points she went on to say, "One has to be competitive on the global arena turf, be ready to compete with every one, from any part of the world and for everything. The global business arena is a global battleground as well as a global melting pot and meeting ground for global collaborative efforts. One can sit back and grumble or make the best use of the opportunities offered by globalisation. The options to whine or win are there for all. It is also a competitive arena to test one's managerial, leadership and entrepreneurial skills."

"It is kaleidoscopic. Each turn brings forth a new setting — a kaleidoscope that keeps on shifting and unfolding diverse perspectives. Shifts during the recent past have been unprecedented. Also, one's viewpoint depends on one's point-of-viewing. It is good. It is bad. It creates new hope. It generates despair. It helps extend goodwill. It causes ill will. It makes people happy. It makes people sad. It invokes envy. It creates affection. It creates employment. It creates unemployment. It creates cyber-global communities. It creates communal conflicts on the ground. It creates prosperity. It generates poverty, as well as disparity. It increases as well as decreases the gaps between haves and have-nots. It benefits. It harms. It brings about inter-cultural understanding, as well as cultural conflicts and divides. It is evolving a seamless world and also creating a fractured global village. It brings out the best as well as the worst side of human beings. I really do not know what to make of it. At times, I feel globalisation is a dynamic mix of xenophobia and transnational goodwill. Frankly I find it hard to give a single, resolved view on globalisation," said a senior international business consultant.

"Globalisation is all pervasive. It is multifaceted. It is a continuous process. Notwithstanding the recent trauma, the new phase of globalisation is in progress. It has political, economical, technical, cultural, and commercial as well as local business perspective. By itself, it is neither good nor bad. It depends on our ability to play the game of globalisation. I feel this is equally true for individuals, corporations and nations. We have to choose our destination on the global landscape. We have to create our own road map to our selected destination. We have to learn to manage the new evolving fault lines; bridge the global divides; harmonise geo-politics and facilitate appropriate shifts in the global power bases," said a professor of international economics.

After explaining some points, he went on to say, "Some economists think of trade and international business as creative destruction. Globalisation is a multidimensional and multifaceted activity. Just as globalisation, global business and market economy has created a web of mutual interests; it has also initiated formation of social landmines in many parts of the world. We have to ask and find answers to questions such as, how much globalisation does a country need? How much globalisation can we digest? How much globalisation should we have? At what pace? Why? For whose benefit? How do we see ourselves? As a part of the global landscape, how or what do we want to be seen as? What role do we want to play on the global stage? Why? What do we want from the world? Why? What do we want to offer the world? Why? And many more such questions."

After further elaborations on some points, he concluded with the observation, "There is a human side of globalisation. Besides various other concerns, globalisation process would bring fore issues such as, conflicts between the rich and poor individuals as well as nations; conflicts between corporate interests and national interests; conflicts between short-term political interests and long-term national interests; as well as conflicts between business and corporate leaders and other stakeholders. Globalisation dividends are unevenly distributed. For sustainable globalisation, we need to ensure equity-oriented globalisation and economic growth." He concluded his discussion, with the observation: "Notwithstanding the new evolving fault lines and constantly growing global divides, I strongly feel, globalisation is an opportunity to learn and attract corporations with skills, technologies and value-adding business processes from different parts of the world."

"Globalisation — it all depends on when, where and with whom you are discussing the subject and in which context. There are proponents as well as opponents of globalisation. There are winners and losers. Every country and community has its share of Marx and market worshipers. Some see very dark clouds while others see bright silver linings. The perspectives change drastically. It can be a very personal, emotional and explosive issue. It has social, economic, ethical, political, cultural as well as technological implications. It is a feeling, an experience, a perception. Some well-informed people earnestly eulogise it as well as fervently condemn it, depending on what aspect of it they are discussing, where, with whom and when. Some see it as a global knitting of the corporate supply chains, while others perceive it as a disintegration of national economic systems. There is a discernable disconnect between hyped aspirations, ground realities and acceptable values. The flat world has many bleeding edges, a variety of facets; some are not so friction friendly or firmly fastened yet," said a senior globetrotter business player.

After elaborating on some of her observations she went on to say, "Whatever one's perceptions of globalisation, it is no longer a question of good or bad, advantages and disadvantages. The imperatives are clear. We have to learn to compete with the most competitive in the global business arena. We have to find ways to transform our operational disadvantages into advantages; make our odds into evens. It is a game of business survival — survival of the fittest. Today, there is no escape from competition." After further discussions she concluded with the observation, "Good or bad, globalisation is a reality. Individuals, corporations and countries have to proactively, innovatively and creatively optimise their own gain-pain equations."

"To understand the process of globalisation, I feel, we have to understand the working equation or geo-politics of citizens, corporations and countries. Given the global connectivity, each one of them wants to feel important and powerful. Each one has an ego and emotions. Citizens as consumers, voters and employees want to feel they control the corporations and countries. Corporations as owners of resources, technology, production capacities feel they can manage the markets. Governments governing the countries feel they are the ultimate rulers. Each is trying to maximise social, economic and political gains from globalisation. The power equations are different in different countries and dynamic in nature. The power equations are local, regional, as well as global. Some individual citizens are more powerful than some nations," said a professor of political science.

After elaborating on some of his concepts he went on to say, "Besides the obvious physical power, power is a perception. It is tacit and implicit. Depending on the national governance system, citizens, corporations and countries exercise their power in different ways, at different times, in different countries. Trends and the impact of globalisation are influenced by these changes. Citizens as consumers and workers impact corporations. Corporations through their public relation strategies try to influence the governors of countries and international institutions. Governments use their policy processes and instruments to achieve their objectives. The dynamics of all these activities impacts the trends in globalisation."

"As the global economy shifts from material resource-based growth to knowledge-based growth, I see tremendous opportunity for developing countries. But, we have to prepare for it in earnest. And the road map would have to be based on education, appropriate education and job-focused talent development," said a senior human resource manager of a large corporation. After some elaborations, he went on to say, "The world is creating opportunities as well as threats at an unprecedented pace and scale. We need to develop our responses at individual, corporate and national levels."

"Self-interest is the principal force behind globalisation. Individuals, corporations and nations cross borders for their own benefit. Over the years, be it armies, adventurers, religious preachers or traders, they have all crossed over national borders with their own objectives. The basic objectives of globalisation remain the same, only the context keeps changing. Individuals as well as corporations cross over national boundaries to maximise their own gains. Corporations go across national boundaries with their own agenda, for their own economic advantages, not with any altruistic motives. We must learn to optimise our individual, corporate and national interests by taking advantage of the available global opportunities. Each gain is situational and has a lifecycle. It is for us to maximise our benefits from these associations. We need to take an appropriate, long-term, sustainable strategic view. I do not believe in selfless charity. Even charity is done for some selfish motives — benefits in this life or the next," said a CEO of a fast-growing media organisation.

After some elaborations he went on to say, "Confusion and conflicts often arise because different cultures and communities interpret self-interest differently. Virtues, vices and values of capitalism are not appreciated equally by all individuals. The issues are further emotionalised when the competitors in the business arena are not seen as equals and the rules are perceived to favour the powerful."

Speaking on similar lines, chief medical officer of a global health care unit said, "When I juxtapose globalisation — competition, deals on the golf course, lavish living of CEOs, public relation events in expensive resorts and hotels, I become a bit suspicious about the rhetoric of hypercompetition in the global arena. Is it really performance in a competitive environment or public relations? A planned drama of competition between two famous global soft drink companies — same quality, same price and same taste, with just divided and demarcated monopolistic markets."

"Globalisation offers many dynamic and diverse opportunities for corporations — opportunities to learn, share, co-operate, compete, grow and diversify. I feel we need to develop each global relationship in its appropriate perspective. Relationships with major global economic bases need to be developed individually. We will have to balance our dependent-independent equation with each one. We have a lot to learn, share and co-operate as well as develop our competitive capabilities, working with each one of them. Also, we need to give each region and country in the world an appropriate and individual attention. Like individuals, each country is different and has multifaceted aspirations. Our business schools, universities and business associations need to develop their own global domain specialisations.

Globalisation is an opportunity for us all," said a professor of economics.

"Globalisation creates connectivity as well as clashes of value and cultures. It promotes creativity as well as conformity. It creates competition and also destroys competition as well as competitors. It gives new emotional and sentimental impetus to individual identities, consumer perceptions and national aspirations. It expands competitive space and also provides opportunities for strategic alliances and learning. It is a mixed bag of creative destruction as well as destructive creativity, challenges and opportunities, competition and learning. We should not expect everybody to have the same view of globalisation, as it affects different segments of society differently," said a lady CEO in the fashion industry.

After elaborating on some points she went on to say, "The simplicity of good and bad in the global village, I often find very scary and frightening. Who is good? Why? Who is bad? Why? What is good about good and what is bad about bad, is often very fuzzy; I am really confused."

"Globalisation. The world seems to be disintegrating. Notwithstanding all the hype, the so-called global village is being divided into demarcated rich lush zones separated by vast economically arid lands. It is creating horizontal and vertical divides. Take a close look at the national and global economic landscape. Globalisation is creating a global volcano. It is not a win-win but a gain-pain equation. It is a world of discord and disharmony. Even global economic institutions such as the World Bank and WTO are full of national politics," said an entrepreneur CMD of a pharmaceutical company. After some discussion he concluded, "We are creating many social time bombs around the world."

Expressing views on similar lines a senior professor said, "Globalisation? It has been around for centuries. Only its form, intensity, visibility and impact have changed.

However, social, economic and political interests are too local to be regionalised or globalised. Employment is a core social, economic and political issue. In democratic market economies, one cannot go to voters and say that one unemployed worker of his area or country is equal to two of another. Sooner or later harsh realities of market economy will hit home. The unpleasant side of market mechanism will hurt the local political interests. Do we have self-sacrificing voters? Where? In which country? We have to wait for a real global recession to test the strength of the global economic bonds and goodwill."

He concluded with the observation, "Corporations want consumers to spend, spend and spend. Also, the same corporations want the same consumers, who are also their workers to work, work and work."

"Globalisation is just another name for corporate colonisation; colonisation of our minds and lifestyles. Almost all democratic market economies today are governed by the governments of corporations, governments by corporations and governments for corporations. What is good for corporations is good for the country, is the prevailing guiding philosophy of market economy governance. Media, our main source of information, is also controlled by corporations. Globalisation is the global spread of corporate culture. Reforms are considered good if they help corporations. Labour laws are good if they help investors. With globalisation our lives are more and more controlled by corporations. What is good to wear, eat, drink, enjoy and also not enjoy is told to us by corporations. Directly or indirectly, even what we should think or not think about is told to us by corporations. Mass media is itself a part of the corporate world. It is a corporate media. Profitability and survival of publications depends on advertisements. Corporations are advertisers. Thus publications dance to the tune of advertisers. Readers like other customers are taken for granted. For sustainable social harmony, we need to promote the concept of principle-based profits in our business culture," said a retired editor of a daily newspaper.

After elaborating on some points he went on to say, "There is a major disconnect between mass media, the masses and mass reality. Mass media I feel serves a very limited social purpose. News is often selected for its money value returns. Market-oriented news gets priority."

After further explaining some of his points he went on to say, "With globalisation, small budding entrepreneurs are ruthlessly annihilated by large, local and transnational corporations. Like individuals, corporations also do crimes. They often create anti-consumer conspiracy and commit oligopolic and monopolistic crimes. Large corporations use money, muscle and mercenary power to make way for their sales in the new markets."

"I feel globalisation has many different perspectives. It has many faces. In fact it has dynamic morphing versatility. It impacts head and heart differently at different times and under different situations. It has various social, political, economic and cultural faces. Each face has its own situational, contextual and time-frame dynamics. It is creating creative groups. It is creating destructive groups. It is providing global connectivity and also isolating individuals. It is destroying values and also giving rise to new ideologies. Frankly I do not know what to make of it," said the CEO of an international NGO.

After elaborating on some points he said, "It is too vast a subject and too complex to be discussed in this short meeting. From your management and management education perspective, I feel we need a new perspective. Management issues have acquired new dimensions. We need new management thinking; a new management philosophy; new rules and regulations for markets as well as resource sharing; and new rules of institutional governance. Globalisation is creating a new world, generating new aspirations." After elaborating on some more points, he went on to say,

"Notwithstanding all the prosperity we see around, I feel, we are going to have shortages of all resources, products and services. The relative prosperity exists for small groups of people and it may be for a limited time. Everything has a lifecycle. When the empowered masses demand their share, will we have resources for all?"

"Capitalism is basically a game of self-interest. Notwithstanding all the rhetoric about the virtues of globalisation, privatization and economic reforms, it is done to promote 'corporatisation' — benefit few selected individuals and corporations. For globalisation to be sustainable, it would have to help flatten the social and economic pyramids in individual countries," said a senior NGO executive.

"Globalisation is a multifaceted activity with multidimensional implications happening on a variety of time scales. Globalisation also tends to disrupt historical trends and activate elements of ideology, self-esteem and national pride. Like other social, economic and political processes, it impacts each individual as well as the strata of society in a different way. Thus the confusion is often initiated or added on by the six-blind-men and the elephant syndrome," said a professor of economics.

"Unlike earlier globalisation processes, this is a globalisation with a difference. Earlier people left their homes to go around the world; now the world comes to their homes. One can now stay at home and work in many different countries, study or teach in different parts of the world or build global relationships. There is a virtual world of instant connectivity for work, trade, learning and entertainment," said the CEO of a dotcom company.

"Globalisation to me is emergence of the world economy as an integrated economic system. The old developed economies of USA, Europe and Japan are emerging as consumers. China is the emerging industry product producer for the world and India is emerging as the back office service provider. Integrated global economy is emerging slowly. The energy suppliers to the world economy, Russia and the countries of the Middle East will also become integrated in the global economic system. We need to pay special attention to countries in Africa and Latin America," said a senior professor of a business school.

Giving a historical perspective of globalisation, a senior partner of a global business consulting organisation said, "The current globalisation movements, I feel, are different from the earlier ones in the sense that those were politic-national expansions. The current global fabric is mainly being woven by technology and corporations. Both are dynamic and adaptive for their own sake, for their own survival and growth. Many corporations earn more from global markets than from their own local, national markets. They are becoming more and more nation-neutral for their sustainable growth. Business leaders are becoming more and more sensitive to sentiments and aspirations of citizens and consumers of different national markets. With time we will see a global network of truly global corporations—as good global corporate citizens with global human values."

"Globalisation is an existing reality, a living experience," said a senior vice-president in the hospitality industry." He continued, "I am amazed, how can anyone question it? The variations in the lifestyles of urban middle class in different countries are narrowing down. Globally, the values, outlook and conversation topics, even the expressions or jargons are also almost similar. Cell phones, music, movies, fashion, brands, credit cards, cars, global-local celebrities, food joints, advertisements, shopping malls and stock market performances are increasingly becoming the common café-conversation topics, with similar accented jargons, gestures and attitudes, around the world."

He went on to elaborate, "It is not just that the services in high-priced hotels in different parts of the world or different international airlines are alike; also, the value systems, social life, entertainment methods, format of many popular TV reality shows and general aspirations of middle and upper classes are similar. In spite of the large variations in the levels of prosperity, there are common status symbols around the world. The evolving global culture is a dynamic market-corporate-product service led culture, and not the tradition-society-nation led culture."

Expressing his views on similar lines, the senior vice-president of a global information technology company said, "Technologies have been developed by corporations for their own benefits. It is to be expected that these technologies be employed to serve corporate objectives in their national and international markets. It is also natural that these technologies and software products be used by corporations to lock-in their customers. The global corporations are carving out the world into their areas of influence."

After elaborating on his observations he continued, "Corporations are commercial entities. It may not be wrong to say that using their global resources, money power, global networks, corporate-political nexus, technology leads, product-service options and marketing strategies, the corporations will increasingly play a more significant role in the day-to-day life of citizens of different countries and also influence values in their favour. A big business political nexus is well known around the world. If we examine our daily product-service consumption patterns, we will get a good feel of the way our lives are being influenced by different corporate brands from different countries. "

"To have a meaningful dialogue, we need to understand the undercurrents of globalisation. When we use simple theories of international trade involving two goods and two countries, it is very easy to see how there is mutual benefit from trade. However, as we make our model more realistic by adding unique characteristics of factors such as labour, capital, brand-equity, intellectual property rights (IPR), productivity and technology levels, the perspective begins to get murky. Globalisation may or may not be beneficial in all cases or for all segments of society. Each country and each industry has to protect its own interests," said a professor of international trade.

After elaborating on his points he went on to say, "The future is more likely to unfold in a non-linear fashion. We have to be sensitive to the new competitive imperatives. At times globalisation seems to be too creamy; led by few companies and few products for a selected few. I do not feel very comfortable about its sustainability. I feel we need to give the globalisation process more local and deeper roots. We need to make it more inclusive and urgently bridge the gap between the top and bottom layers of our social and economic pyramid."

After explaining some of his observations he went on to say, "Economic changes create the need for new social and governance structures. Economic growth destroys traditional social frameworks and structures faster than it can create new appropriate ones. There is an urgent need for new and more effective global governance norms and institutions."

"Corporations are guided by their own economic equations and business priorities. As more and more corporations take a global perspective of their operations and try to optimise their global value chains, more and more jobs will shift from one region to another. It will force economically developed countries to get out of their historic social and business comfort zones and adjust to a new global economic framework. To take advantage of the emerging opportunities, developing countries would be competing with each other for global business partnerships with corporations. One would have to prepare a long-term perspective of the world trends, one's own role in it and act accordingly," said a senior lady executive in the pharmaceutical industry.

"As new markets are essential for corporate expansions, globalisation is inevitable. Multiproduct, hi-tech corporations are constantly prowling around the world for resource hunting and market development to improve their bottom line. The economics of global value chains are changing fast. Corporations are increasingly outsourcing, redesigning their business models, and re-engineering their corporate architectures. All this is being done to align corporate operations with their global economic equations. Slowly the global-local mix of corporation in their operations will become dynamically balanced. Local stakeholders will become significant," said a senior executive of a transnational medical equipment manufacturing firm.

Elaborating on similar lines a senior lady professor of political science said, "It is common knowledge that the domestic and multinational corporations have used and will continue to use their political lobbies and leverages in the countries where they operate, to modulate business policies in their favour. Large corporations have become powerful supercitizens or market kings. In the market economy it is not uncommon, in fact, I feel natural, for the presidents and prime ministers to promote interests of their national corporations in the global business arena. Interests of new budding entrepreneurs are often overlooked. We need to take a comprehensive social-political view of the international commercial activities. Today many corporations are larger economic entities than nations."

After some digressions she voiced her concern, "There is little evidence that the corporate world or even political leadership is gifted with a high degree of moral maturity. The technological-industrial-commercial conglomerate merely asks what it can do and not what it should do. Its objective is enhancement of market strength and not upgradation of social welfare, justice or morality. I feel we need to question all assumptions relating to the process of globalisation, such as, what makes good, good, and also what makes bad, bad; for whom, under what circumstances and for how long." She concluded with the remarks, "A flat world is just a façade. I feel it is frivolous and fractured. Self-interest is being promoted with altruistic slogans."

"From our corporate perspective, globalisation is the process of deepening and broadening the base of existing global relationships. It is an action-oriented activity, with very little time to wait and watch. Cost of acquiring new customers is increasing every day. Battering from competition from different, known and unknown global sources is changing the rules of the game. Internal systems as well as customer relations need to be constantly realigned," said the CEO of a global logistics company.

"Whatever our perception of globalisation, I feel, many questions will crop up in our mind as we move towards a greater degree of globalisation. As we move around the marketplace, one cannot but wonder about the global-local mix. Should we worry about it as long as we get world quality products at competitive prices? What national policy frame-work will ensure that we are getting world-class goods at competitive prices? Should a coloured water soft drink be as expensive as milk? Is there competition between coloured water soft drinks that sell the same quantity and the same quality at the same price? On what basis are they competing? Is it all pre-arranged pricing and is the show of competition just a big façade or sham? Is there competition or just mutual market adjustment? One notices similar situations in other products being marketed by multinational corporations. Often I feel I am living in a world of cheating corporations and cheated customers, or to say it diplomatically, deceiving corporations and deceived customers. How are we, as consumers, to protect ourselves from being exploited?" observed a lady senior citizen, a former CEO of an NGO.

"It is said that globalisation and competition go hand-in-hand. Corporations, around the world are not known for fair play. And, who likes competition? Innovative tacit cartels and creative behind-the-scene deals are not uncommon in the business world. Every nation needs an independent business and a competition-monitoring system. We need a competitive environment and a system that ensures fair competition between different business players, where every player, new and old, local and global has a fair chance to compete and also win. I feel we need an independent global body to draw out an effective framework for 'fair-competition' and monitor competition at least for essential products. It may be done as it is done for sports and games. At present, competition in business is a very fuzzy and obscure term," said a retired executive from an international organisation. After some discussions, he concluded with a remark, "How transparent are business activities? Do we really know what is going on in golf courses or the bars of expensive hotels?"

"I think the global business arena is an arena of competition as well as cooperation between the minds of the people. In the global arena it may not be wrong to say that it is the Japanese mind, the German mind, the Mexican mind, the Chinese mind, the American mind or the Indian mind that are in competition with each other. Besides promotion of 'isms' one can also see promotion of cultural-ism in a way that the French are promoting French-ness and the Americans are promoting American-ness. Transnational corporations have nationalities. Most multinational corporations operate in their national ways. No doubt there are cross-cultural teams but it is the individuals that constitute teams. Corporate and business diplomacy is used to bind and knit it all together globally for the benefit of a few limited liability shareholders in their country of origin," said a senior diplomat.

Speaking on the framework to synergise national resources with global commercial trends, a senior civil service executive observed, "We need national level research and academic institutions to analyse the global trends and gain insights of the new global realities. There is a discernable credibility gap between corporations and consumers. The conflict between corporate and social values often disrupts in different parts of the world. Given the increasing size of corporations and their interface with national-social-economic cultural frameworks, we need to empathetically analyse the relationship trends, and create a dialogue forum for both. Numbers of national size corporations are on the rise. We need to understand the new global realities and educate the consumers and public along with even the politicians as well as the future corporate managers."

"I am not a free market fundamentalist. I believe economic forces need to be planned for, carefully directed and monitored, or even controlled. National governments have to protect interests of their citizens and emerging entrepreneurs. Multinational corporations entering a country do so with their own 'selfish' agendas. Corporations are neither democratic nor transparent. Corporations do not like competition. Who does? It is for the governments to ensure free and fair competition in their country that benefits their citizens and new emerging entrepreneurs," said a senior global business consultant. He concluded with the statement, "You will get many perceptions of globalisation. I feel none would be wrong. However the observations may suffer from perceptive deficiencies. The perceptions may be one-dimensional — the dimension of the perceiver. I have my perception, my dimension."

"Globalisation has increased the zones of competition. Today there is competition between nations, corporations and individuals. We need to improve our efficiency standards in every phase of our social, economic and political life. We have to learn to manage our individual and social resources effectively. Given our large population, social disparities and limited resources, we need to critically examine our ways of using our available resources. Management has to become a national religion for us. We need to critically examine our resource management methods and policies. Every citizen must be made aware of his responsibilities as a manager-citizen," said a former senior lady executive.

"All sales are local. Sales are the lifelines of corporations. Thus for local and multinational business organisations to grow, they need to comprehensively understand local business practices. It is here that the B-schools need to deepen their roots," said the CEO of a large retail organisation.

After some digression and elaborations he went on to say, "Given our historical advantages of cultural tolerance, we can aspire to become the most value-based global value chain link for multinational corporations. Corporations are always in the process of realigning and re-engineering their corporate structures to optimise economics of their global value chain. We can offer a value based, value adding competitive hub for their global business models."

"Globalisation is a no-option imperative. To compete or not to compete is not an option any more; all globalisation is local. To be effective, globalisation needs local roots. Taking this into account, to optimise their value-addition options, the B-schools need to re-orient their local-global orientation," said the former country head of a MNC consultancy organisation.

After some elaborations he went on to say, "There are good reasons to love globalisation and there are also equally good reasons to hate globalisation. We need to understand the process in a sensitive and holistic way. We need to balance the global-local social, economic and cultural equations." He concluded with the statement, "Democracies as well as markets have to become more sensible and global business more sensitive for harmonious growth of globalisation."

As we discussed the concepts of management and globalisation with people from different walks of corporate life, it became evident that there was an awareness as well as concern — awareness about the diverse fast-paced changes, concern about the state of the art of management and management education, its capabilities and its competencies to cope with changes and emerging challenges. This motivated us to gain some understanding and insight of the nature of the global business arena.

3

The Global Business Arena

"Competition, more competition and still more competition, that is what the global business arena is all about," said the CEO of a medium size international consultancy organisation.

"It is a corporate war zone. Like any other war zone, it is an arena where winning matters. Business wars are fought for winning customers or capturing purchasing power of customers. Customers are won over for generating profits. Brands are used as reliable and attractive value offers to win over customers and generate business relationship loyalties. Brands are also used as bombs, bullets and bayonets to keep off competitors," said a senior vice-president of a large FMCG company.

"The global business arena is dynamic, fuzzy, foggy and at times an explosively xenophobic, commercial war zone. A commercial war is a war for customers. But customers are an enigma, to say the least. The irony of the situation is that customers are no one other than people like you and me; you and me in the real and virtual markets — bazaars, *haats*, shopping malls, over the phones or on the net. All these are close hand-to-hand war zones. Yet we become so unpredictable, complex and impulsive when it comes to selecting a product or a service. Thus the customers as targets are dynamic and illusive. Individually and as a segment, they keep changing their preferences. Thus the business arena becomes a zone of rivalry, warfare, strategic thinking, determination and resilience," said the lady CMD of a publishing company.

After elaborating on some of her observations she went on to say, "Who really controls the critical global resources, technologies, knowledge bases and skill sets? How is the overall global economic pie divided? Who is competing with whom? For what? Why? I really do not know." She concluded with the observation, "The global business arena is in urgent need of a framework for fair competition — a globally credible transnational business competition framework along with a globally credible governance framework."

"It is an arena of competition and conflicts. The local-global conflict is present in almost every human interaction. It has various tones of social, economic, cultural and political dimensions. The dynamics of nationalities, loyalties, patriotism and affiliations provide kaleidoscopic views," said the lady CEO of a large travel agency. After some elaborations she went on to say, "Frankly I feel, the only way for a nation to be and remain competitive is by developing its manpower — developing effective talent pools. Keeping in view the fast-changing environment, one has to be a proactive learner. Successful executives are busy learning themselves; they don't have time to teach. There is competition for everything, at every level — individual, corporate, social and national."

"To me the business arena is a zone of dream wars, battles and skirmishes. Corporations sell dreams — dreams of happiness, satisfaction and a good life. Customers are in search of their dreams and they buy their dreams. Dreams that fulfil expressed as well as unexpressed desires. Corporations are competing with each other to sell more satisfying dreams. Corporations create a vision around their products and services. A product or a service can be so many different things to different people. Some visions are created by corporations; others are created by customers themselves. We are the creators and consumers, as customers we pay for those visions. Brands to me have dream-satisfying qualities associated with the names of the products; an aura of vision and values," said a lady CEO in jewellery business.

"Corporations sell value; value in the form of products and services. Corporations transform raw inputs into higher value outputs. The challenges and the conflict or war in the business arena is on the credibility and claims which different organisations make about their value propositions. Customers look for bargains in the marketplace. They want maximum value for their money. I feel the business arena is all about credible value claims by products and services. After all a value is a value only when it is perceived as a value by the person who has to value the value," said the CEO of a large fashion house.

"The business arena is a zone of lies, lies and more lies. Perhaps, I should add, a competitive zone of creative lies or sugar-coated lies. Show me a single business advertisement that tells the truth. Business organisations tell lies about the products they sell and the kind of jobs they offer. In the business arena, companies compete on the basis of their abilities to tell lies in creative and credible ways. Also, often corporations sell unethical promises using unethical means," were the views of a CEO of an NGO.

"Global business arena — I feel every market, every shop and every sales shelf is a competitive global business arena today. Products or brands of corporations from different parts of the world are often presented at their best, to gain customer attention, on the same shelf, same shop or in the same shopping malls. Success or failure of products is decided in these competition zones. However, why one brand is a success in one arena and a failure in another is always a mystery. For some the world may be flat, but globalising products and services has many highs and lows, successes as well as failures. Many suppositions are developed after the results. That is what makes business an interesting game of perpetual uncertainties. Globality is a complex, multifaceted operation," said a CEO in the footwear industry.

"Today the global arena is a very complex business, social and cultural arena. Agricultural, industrial and knowledge economies are all dynamically mixed. Processing of raw materials, ideas and information are happening concurrently. Business economics of increasing returns exist alongside those of diminishing returns. Economics of processing bulk goods differs from crafting knowledge into products. Nature of competition is different in different industries. Global-local ingredients are different. Each requires different sets of knowledge bases, skill sets and strategic thinking. I find it difficult to make a meaningful general statement about the global business arena," said a global business consultant. After some elaborations he went on to say, "We are in an era of unprecedented innovations, disruptions and transformations. There are constant disruptions and transformations because of creative and innovative uses of technology, business models, leadership and business processes."

"To be frank, when I lean back and close my eyes, I cannot help but smirk. We are one of the leading players in the global arena, in India and abroad, when it comes to creating competition. Competition is in the mind, not in the market. We create images, slogans, value propositions for customers we know little about. We talk of brands, without really knowing what a brand is really all about. Of course it is a name, but what else? I feel like a priest in the temple who sells God without knowing who God is or whether one exists. He gives names to different Gods. We do the same. I guess that is what we call *maya* or even *mithiya*. But our clients and their customers believe in what we say. I guess, at the end of the day, that is what really matters," said the creative director of a large advertising agency.

After some digressions and detailed discussions over some cups of coffee, he went on to say, "I have been in this business for over a quarter of a century; I enjoy it but I really, really do not know what I am doing. I have won awards for creativity and have been given credit for creating brands. But, what is a brand, I really do not know. What makes a brand good, weak or sick, I do not know. Since you have asked me a frank question, I want to be honest with you. I am enjoying what I am doing. It is called creativity. But what am I doing, I really do not know. Just as I have been given credit for success, I am sure I would have caused many failures also; killed some brands, by wrong creativity and wrong advertisements. But we are not supposed to talk about that."

"I feel the global business arena is an arena of corporate conflicts. But what does winning and losing mean in the global arena. Who wins? Who loses? Individuals, corporations, stakeholders or nations? Who gains and who loses when a large corporation replaces hundreds of small aspiring entrepreneurs? What are social, economic and cultural trade-offs when a local corporation in a developing country is taken over by a large transnational corporation? Are there inherent conflicts between corporate finance and microfinance? Is it possible to synergise aspirations of large corporations and aspirations of the little entrepreneurs? Why do people not object when small units are taken over by big corporations? Is it just a simple rule of nature that big fish have a right to eat small fish — might is right? If I sound confused, it is because I am confused," said the owner of a retail outlet.

"The global business arena is an arena of competitive-idea managers and opportunity managers. Each individual is a customer — an opportunity. However, each individual is really an individual and has to be handled as an individual. As in cricket, each ball has to be played on its own merits. I feel the success in the business arena comes in small steps. It is based on how we handle each customer. It is a competitive relationship-building game. It is a game of transforming a casual customer into a long-term association. For us, I feel it is a one-customer-at-a-time game," said a senior manager in the manufacturing industry.

"You may be surprised, but I think of the global business arena like a crowded dance hall; a dance hall where the music keeps changing unexpectedly. To keep pace one has to keep changing one's steps and body movements," said a senior professional in the entertainment industry. After some elaborations he went on to say, "At times the global business arena also seems to resemble an innovative fast-paced, multi-star action movie."

"I feel the future corporate wars in the global business arena will be technology based. Inability to cope with new or disruptive technologies would lead to a loss of business. The banking operations nowadays are technology dependent. We are in the transactional service industry. The products, services and processes in our industry are well defined. Take the example of a credit card; it is all technology. Technology-driven ATMs, for all practical purposes, are our critical customer relationship and customer interface managers. We need to make them more customer friendly," said a senior bank manager.

After discussing some details, he went on to say, "To compete, we need people who understand and can appreciate the role of technology in customer relations, are skilled in technology or are fast learners of technology, and also have soft skills to empathise with non-technical customers. Our critical success factor, as I see it, is a reliable courteous service. Banking, I feel is more a game of skills and attitude rather than a knowledge base. We work with well-defined processes that are technology based. Even if someone were to give me an innovative idea of a new product or service, I will just have to forward it to head office. All meaningful major changes are done after very serious considerations at the top. That is where we need a few experienced knowledge workers with extensive domain knowledge; people who can analyse and provide solutions to the business problems. Knowledge, as I see it, is the ability to appreciate and define the problem in our overall domain context and skill is the ability to provide acceptable value addition along with customer-focused and customer-friendly solutions."

After some elaboration he went on to say, "We need goal or target-oriented innovations. We cannot leave it to chance to happen. We need to be target specific with insights of cost and revenue streams. Business economics is the main strategic guiding factor. It gives us the blue print for the future."

"Business is a competitive techno-economic operation. Profits are generated by adding value to raw materials at a minimum cost. Being in the transformation industry, the value comes from transforming raw materials into value-added goods. The challenge is to do it at a minimum cost while maintaining or improving quality. For us, innovation or improvement has meaning only if it can cut cost or increase revenue. Thus for every innovative proposal, the questions are the same — will it help us get higher revenue from the same customers or from a new set of customers? Will it reduce our cost? I feel this is how it may be in other industries also. After all, all businesses are in search of ways to improve margins; increase the difference between revenue and cost, through kaizen or innovations; serving the same customers more effectively; or exploring for a new segment of customers."

After elaborating on the above concepts, the CEO of a metal processing unit went on to say, "Like competitive individuals, corporations too in the global arena are constantly fighting wars on two fronts: internal, to improve internal efficiencies, and external to improve relations with customers to keep up or do better than their competitors.

On the global scale, one has to cope with internal diversity of corporate personnel, technology and systems while on the external front it is the new business environment and cross-cultural customers with their own perceptions and expectations. We operate in a specialised and well-demarcated B2B niche segment."

"The global business arena is a learning arena. The learning curves are short and steep. We have to learn to be geo-economic, geo-political, geo-cultural, geo-business savvy and smart," said the CEO of an international travel business unit.

"We are in the knowledge era with instant global connectivity. Our clients, operating in various industries around the world, expect us to have the most current information about their domains. They expect us to be able to understand their problems from their perspective, to provide appropriate solutions to improve their performance, or explore new growth options. Our professional competence is in getting most recent, reliable and relevant information for analysis and developing alternate solutions in the least possible time. Knowledge after all is the competency to provide effective solutions. We are always on the look out for people, who know their limits but are willing to learn; have intellectual empathy as well as curiosity; are proactive learners; have the ability to ask appropriate questions; are active listeners; can assimilate data quickly and come up with alternate options; and are able to effectively communicate with their clients. The list may look long, but frankly it is all included in the package of an enthusiastic business player," said a senior partner of an international business consultancy organisation.

After some elaborations he went on to explain, "For us to survive in the hypercompetitive global arena, constant learning, unlearning and relearning are professional imperatives. Also, being proactive in understanding the clients' current and future growth directions are critical for our sustainable growth. I would say our battle zones with our competitors would be in the knowledge bank as well as in our credibility, commitment and concern for our clients."

After some discussions on various-related subjects he went on to say, "There has been a lot of talk about positioning India on the global business arena. I strongly feel that India should use its diversity to its advantage and let its positions evolve at different levels in different segments in the global arena. For its own advantages, India needs different images and perceptions in different social, economic, cultural and political global arenas. Each industry needs different images, be it entertainment or health care, education or tourism."

"Notwithstanding all the talk and hype about hypercompetition in the global business arena, I feel, the global business arena is full of inefficiencies and ineffectiveness. Based on my personal experience with some leading global corporations, I can say that there is a major disconnect between the nature of jobs, skills required for the specific jobs, and the appointments. Job-MBA mismatch is a common observation. In most of the industries, be it transactional, transformational or tacit knowledge intensive, we need a few specialists and more implementors or workers. But job-specific trained people are not available in the market. Corporations pick from the available lot of education output. Education output streams and industry input needs are out of sync. Thus, there is a large amount of human talent, job-need mismatch leading to tremendous amount of human talent wastage or underutilisation. All this leads to high internal and external process incompetence and high transactional costs," said a senior international human resource consultant.

After elaborating on some of his points he went on to say, "For optimal results we need to ask — how much brainpower or strategic inputs the corporations need? How much technology and human power do the companies need to implement their strategies? What kind of knowledge bases, skill sets and mindsets or attitudes do the companies require for optimal results? I personally feel corporations need a few questioning and strategic brains with a large number of do-as-told implementors at different levels. With the help of computers and sophisticated software, large amounts of work can be machine supported. We need to ask, how many managers does a company require? Given the technology options, we also need to ask about the skill sets required. In most cases, the transnational corporate pyramid has a small top but a big base spread in many countries."

"For some jobs, the global business arena is an extension of home. Homes are a part of the global cyber world. Add to that the internet-linked mobile phones and laptops. Where are the boundaries between the home and the workplace? The global business arena is an integral part of our modern day speed living, regardless of where we are," said a senior vice-president in the telecommunication industry.

"It is an arena of transnational movement of people, products, services, ideas, brands, information, artefacts, money, images, spirituality, health care, risks, pollution, values, cultures and many other social, economic, political and cultural elements in an organised as well as unorganised way. Most national stock markets have become global casinos," said a senior executive in the music and entertainment industry. After some discussions and comments on the ethics in the global business arena he said, "Just as peace-time ethics and war-time ethics are different, business ethics as discussed in B-school classrooms and ethics of the business arena have little in common."

"It is commonly said that the future corporate wars will be fought for talent. I think there has always been a war for talent. Countries try to attract the best global talent for development of new technologies. Also, good managers have always been in short supply. What I feel is that current corporate wars are and future corporate wars will continue to be for customers — acquiring new customers and improving services to existing customers. Talent is just a means to that end. Talent is an input for developing internal capabilities and competencies. Also, talent to be effective has to match corporate objectives and job requirements. Thus talent as a word is not an operational word. It is too general." After elaborating on some of his concepts, the CEO of a placement agency said, "To perform a job effectively, one needs an appropriate mix of knowledge base, skill sets and mindset or attitude. Each job has its own unique requirements. When we speak of talent — in general not operational terms — at serious business forums, we do more harm than good. To be action oriented we have to be specific that we need specific skill sets for BPOs, KPOs or other kinds of skill-oriented jobs. Particular skills may be critical success factors for some operations, but may be of little use to others."

"Talent is a much hyped term. There is so much wastage of talent as I see it. How many jobs are there in India that require an IIT qualification? Then we go on to add IIM to it. Do we make IIT learning more effective or less and for what kind of jobs? Where are those jobs?" observed a senior investment banker. He went on to elaborate, "Today near-perfect financial statements can be prepared by feeding published inputs into computers. Very effective software has been developed in the recent past. We usually operate in limited-option business situations; options usually specified by clients. Computers using sophisticated software usually guide us to the solution. Clients also tend to trust computer outputs. Jobs requiring human judgements are not expanding in most industries. Today, I feel what the industry needs is some specific skills with an attitude to enjoy routine. We compete with specific talents, technology-based systems, relationships, smiles and customer concerns."

After a short pause to elaborate on his views, he went on to say, "How many brilliant decision makers does a global investment bank need? I am talking of investment banks because I have been associated with one for the past two decades. I am one of the many IIT-IIMs working here. Please do not ask me how often and what jobs I really do to keep myself occupied. Frankly, I feel, to win the corporate wars, what the bank needs is enthusiastic employees and not stressed out engineering brilliance."

Another IIT-ISB educated senior business executive working in a leading FMCG-MNC observed, "We have to face the realities of the business world; we have to learn to enjoy the job we do. It is like an arranged marriage. Frankly, I feel, in reality there are no so-called dream jobs in most industries. Every job has to get routine after a while. If the money is good we have to just learn to enjoy the job. As for corporate wars, one does not need brilliance to win market wars. From my experience with an MNC, I feel money and muscle power is often more effective than brainpower."

"Well you may call me a corporate warrior — a corporate warrior in the global business arena. I feel like a mercenary, fighting a marketing war for a multinational company," said a senior executive of an MNC.

After some deliberations on his statements, he went on to say, "People talk of loyalty and commitment in the business arena. I often wonder, loyalty to whom? Why and for what? As a professional I feel, I should be loyal to myself, my family, my profession and my career."

Addressing the same issue from another perspective, the country head of an MNC said, "Multinational or transnational corporations are still in the evolutionary process. The companies are still known by the nation of their origin. They are headquartered in their nation of origin, primarily governed by their national laws, like to hold absolute controlling stake in their foreign operations or to impose their management processes, structures and thinking along with their national brands on global markets. National values and cultural traits dominate the corporate work methods and corporate social culture. The spirit of globalisation is missing; thus, for another national to feel like a commercial target-focused mercenary is natural. The spirit of global-corporate citizenship with local socio-economic commitments and concerns is yet to evolve. Most MNCs still have a short-term perspective on their global operations, especially in Asia. Sometimes the trend seems to be in the other direction. To cope with imperatives of competition, in many of their operations, MNCs are becoming less transparent. In the long run, to optimise on their global resources and synergise local, social, as well as political support, I feel MNCs will evolve as a global corporate citizen governance framework. It will enhance commitment of its personnel from different nationalities to the global corporate objectives."

After sharing some of his experiences and views on the subject, he went on to say, "Complex global corporate structures are being designed to evolve global corporate citizenship structures. The issue of a global-local mix is in a state of flux for most organisations. Corporations are in the process of evolving their global values, concerns, and perspectives. I feel B-schools should try to develop a futuristic perspective in that direction. Developing a working framework and a road map for evolution of global corporate citizenship would be a challenging agenda for business leaders and scholars."

"I think the Olympic motto — *Citius, Altius, Fortius* which means swifter, higher, stronger can be applied to the global business arena also. Business wars are fought on many fronts simultaneously. We need a global framework for corporate competition — a credible fair competition. The global fabric is being woven by global corporate networks. We need an effective and inclusive framework where national citizens become effectual stakeholders of global corporations; credible and involved partners in mutually beneficial local development projects," said a former sports star in the sports and celebrity promotion business.

"I feel the global business arena is in a dynamic evolutionary stage. Frankly I am not even sure what form it will take in the future. I would not even want to guess. There are too many variables and trends — some visible, some invisible; some apparent, some hidden. Similarly there are many big opportunities, small opportunities, visible opportunities, invisible opportunities ready to be exploited. Who will exploit which opportunity, it is hard to say. Similarly there are many risks and hazards on the way to globalisation — some obvious, some dormant," said the senior executive of a large IT company.

After sharing his experiences in different parts of the world he went on to say, "Many nations and parts of the world are still to occupy their due and potential positions on the global stage. The future, I feel would not be a linear projection of the past or even present trends. We have to deal with the world the way it really is; not in the way it should be in our perception. Notwithstanding all the hype about a borderless world, the nation of origin is an emotional anchor and an identity for individuals. There are many very disturbing trends. The social and economic disparities in many parts of the world are moving towards explosive situations. Our own growth model is promoting disparities. I feel we need more inclusive social orientation. At times there is rhetoric but little sustained effort in that direction. If timely action is not taken, the global business arena may evolve into a lawless jungle with many social landmines."

"The global business arena is a global arena of learning. I often think it is a global *gurukul*. I feel, as we have access to global learning sources on every subject, the onus of learning is on us, as individuals. This is an epoch of innovations and new ideas. To be ill-informed in the current knowledge era would be a big disadvantage for every individual, more so as the world economy and commercial scenario is becoming more complex and dynamic. For our personal as well as career growth, Internet and other media provide us many useful and effective cross-cultural and international learning sources. I strongly feel that more and more corporations and educational institutes should make use of global learning sources to enhance cross-cultural learning and understanding of global issues," said a former director of a B-school, currently an active senior citizen.

"Notwithstanding all the hype about globalisation, as far as business is concerned, all corporate wars are local. As in other war situations, knowledge of local business landscape and local business culture, business sense and business thinking is essential. Also it is critical to have an understanding of the local customer mind. Corporate warriors to be effective need to be well versed with local business ethos and customer perceptions," said the former senior vice-president of a global business consultancy organisation.

The perceptions of global business arena vary. We expected it. However, what was often obvious was that the differences, as we perceived, were not just due to the differences in vintage points but often intrinsic to the viewer. The questions which often cropped up in our minds during the interactions related to the perceptions of challenges and opportunities in the global business area as perceived by different business players.

4

Challenges and Opportunities

"Performance. Consistent performance. Higher performance. Consistently higher performance. Doing more with less. The challenges are to reach the global performance standards in whatever we do and then excel. That is the challenge future managers will face everywhere — in every job, in every industry. Challenge is a mindset game. The challenges have to be defined by us, ourselves. It all depends on our own vision of ourselves. Where we want to be? In a competitive environment, performance is all that matters. To survive in the aggressive business world, one has to perform better than competitors," said a lady senior manager in the air-travel industry.

After elaborating on different ways used to evaluate performance in different jobs, she went on to say, "Corporate performance is the sum total of individual performances. Thus, we all have a role in enhancing corporate performance. In this competitive business arena, one cannot afford to relax on any front. Customers have options. Competitors are waiting to exploit even the slightest customer dissatisfaction; the least customer dissatisfaction is a business opportunity for someone else. I feel one can demonstrate one's contribution and competency at every customer-interface point. Also, we are all a link in the overall corporate value chain. Thus, I feel performance in every job matters, all the time."

"As new evolving players on the global stage, our corporations have to face the challenges and utilize the opportunities to define their own role for the global business arena. As global actors they have to become global business-diplomacy savvy. New skills and new global perspectives have to be acquired," said a senior manager in the hospitality industry.

"We live in a corporate era. The challenges and opportunities, as I see, are in evolving a global value-based corporate culture and designing a credible global corporate governance framework. I feel we need corporations with some social cause. Not just profits but profits for a cause; not just for a few shareholders with limited liability ownerships, even if the cause is self-serving through social development," said the CEO of a NGO. After some discussions she went on to say, "Corporations need to have a social conscience. Global corporations need a global conscience. For sustainable inclusive growth, evolving corporations with social concerns and conscience is the challenge."

"I feel, today the opportunities for individuals and corporations in the world are curbed only by the limitations of their imagination. Each industry collectively and each corporation individually should work out its global growth plan. Individual professionals need to work out their own growth plans. Business schools and business associations can pool resources and work together to help industries and individual corporations provide alternate growth plans. These may be in the form of live case studies," said a senior business consultant.

"Today we live in a world full of global opportunities and global challenges. There are no limits. Even sky is not the limit. We need to view obstacles as opportunities. As in games and sports, obstructions are opportunities and challenges in the global business arena. We have many such examples before us. What limits us is our own limitations; levels of our own ambitions; our own desire to excel or achieve. We create our own achievement levels and emotional-comfort zones. Opportunities? There are enough examples of Indian business players captaining transnational corporations," said the lady CMD of a large organisation. After some discussions she said, "The challenges and opportunities are in trying to shape the globalisation process or else we may get shaped by it. The challenge is to control and move towards our self-determined destiny and ensure a rightful place for ourselves, our company and our country in the global arena."

"Opportunity to learn, learn and learn or if stated differently, the need to learn, unlearn and relearn. With round-the-clock instant availability of the Internet and global connectivity, I feel, we have all the opportunity to learn from innumerable global sources on any subject we like. Continuous learning is essential to cope with the fast-changing developments on various technology fronts," said a senior professor of a management and technology institute.

"Globalisation provides great potential and opportunities to leverage synergies in different social, cultural, technological and economic areas. We can learn, share and enrich ourselves in many different ways. Global connectivity and ease in cross-national movements provide us unlimited opportunities to enhance our social, economic and cultural enrichment," said a lady university teacher.

"Diversity management — as Indian corporations venture beyond national boundaries and operate in other countries, Indian executives managing global operations have to learn to effectively deal with a multi-cultural, multi-ethnic and multi-racial workforce; work with diverse technologies in different business environments; as well as deal with individual customers, corporate clients and consumers. The challenge of diversity management has to be accomplished while maintaining global standards of excellence, ethics and compliance," said a senior manager in the transnational information technology organisation.

"Managing the two Ds — diversity and dynamics in the global business arena would be new challenges. Diversity in sources, processes and delivery options; diversity in customers, corporate teams, business suppliers and customer interface options; various diversities in multinational and cross-cultural global supply chains; and dynamics, because everything seems to be in transition. Transition in unexpected ways, in unexpected directions and at an unexpected speed. Both internally and externally, we seem to be operating in a state of dynamic diversity equilibrium," said the vice-president in the international travel industry.

After explaining some nuances, challenges and learning opportunities in cross-cultural business operations, he went on to narrate a learning experience: "During one of the informal interactions over coffee or *gahawa Arabia* with his Arab business partners, the topic of cross-cultural management cropped up. He casually enquired from the Sheikh in his Arab outfit of *Thobe, Ghutra* and *Bisht* and his lady manager wearing *Abaya*, "How would you in your country say 'no' to a business offer." After looking at each other and sharing some thoughts in Arabic the Sheikh replied, "We normally do not say 'no' but may respond by invoking the will of God by saying *Insha-allah*." He went on to elaborate on his response. The lady manager elaborating it further said, "Please note, it is not the invoking the will of God or saying *Insha-allah* that is noteworthy, it is also the way one says it; such as the tone and facial expressions." Then she explained her views using an interesting example. "When my children ask me for something and I say *Insha-allah*, they take note of my facial expression and the tone of my voice and ask me, but *Insha-allah* when — now, today or tomorrow?" she concluded with a smile.

After some discussions on the various learning opportunities in cross-cultural operations, he narrated another example and said that when he asked a similar question from another senior business executive in another country, the reply he got was, "We don't say nothing; we don't hurt no one."

After some further discussions on the subject he concluded with the observations that, "India with so many official languages and cultural variations provides the best platform for cross-cultural learning. Each state has a distinctly different geographic landscape as well as mindscape; also there is a marked difference in business cultures and consumer behaviour in different states as well as within the same state."

"Innovations, more innovations and still more insightful innovations — that is the greatest need and challenge today. The domestic and global business landscape is constantly changing. The future managers will not only have to spot the fuzzy opportunities and translate them into business propositions but also transform them into competitive value-generating business models, in the minimum possible time and most probably with minimal resources. To be meaningful and useful, we need innovations in the given or related business context," said a senior lady manager in the white goods industry.

After some elaborations she went on to say, "New ideas, innovations and opportunities usually present themselves in very crude and abstract forms. At times, even the original perceiver may not be very certain about its value. Translating the new perceived opportunity into a discernable business proposition is usually based on many assumptions. The challenge for future managers would be to assimilate data from relevant reliable sources and create a structure to support their vision for the perceived opportunity in the shortest possible time. Moving with speed while keeping customer focus in developing new products or services would be a challenge for future managers."

Challenges and Opportunities

"In marketplaces, products get morphed into services; and services to be effective need to be individualised. Given the increasing diversity of customers in every market and the number of options before them, the challenge for future business managers will be to make available their product-service mix in keeping with customer preference, in different global markets at different times. Customisation would be a big challenge. Maintaining continuity and incorporating change as well as appropriate diversity in their brands would be a major challenge for them," said a senior marketing manager in the FMCG industry.

"Leadership — self-leadership and leading their teams to serve their customers more profitably would be a major challenge for future managers. I would like to add that building an effective team would itself be a complex challenge. With shifting customer requirements, the need for knowledge bases and skill sets keeps changing. Developing a customer sensitive and customer-focused team in a fast moving business scenario, calls for extraordinary human relations and leadership skills," said a lady partner of a multinational consultancy firm.

She went on to elaborate, "Leadership means different things to different people. Leadership is situational. Each leader has a unique style. In our current business context, leadership to me means ability to guide the growth of a business organisation at a pace faster than the industrial average, with better than industrial average profit margins on a sustainable basis. The challenge for leaders would be to get optimal contribution from each of their team members, in that direction."

After touching upon some related topics she went on to say, "To be meaningful, in business we need a measure to gauge the value of concepts such as innovations or ideas. Given the simple business economics equation, profit is equal to revenue minus cost, I feel we can get a fairly good idea of the value of a suggestion, an innovation or a new idea, or even a disruptive idea by asking simple questions — how will it impact our revenue equation or add to revenue or customer satisfaction? And similarly on the cost side, what are the costs involved? Juxtaposing the two, we can get a fairly good idea of its potential value; just a simple cost-benefit analysis. Does it sound too simple? Try it. Simplicity, I feel is an effective strategy in a complex business situation. Frankly, business is complex, but not as complex as it is often made out to be," she said with a smile.

She concluded with a remark, "Leaders need to communicate their ideas. They need credibility to sustain leadership. For that, I feel leaders need to be simple, like Mahatma Gandhi."

"Having an understanding of the ground realities of the global business arena is critical today. Given the opportunities and advantages of global connectivity, I feel we need to create global linkages for training between corporations and business schools by creating global business games and simulation exercises. With the cooperation of industry, these can be made topical and situation specific to enhance their learning value. Making use of video conferencing, these may be discussed in corporate training centres or business school classrooms with global participation," said a senior human resource manager of a transnational corporation.

"Motivation — keeping oneself motivated to consistently perform effectively in a business organisation, especially multinational organisations would be a challenge for future managers," said a senior vice-president in the auto industry.

After elaborating on his fast career growth in the industry, he went on to say, "What is there for a person to keep going in a corporate setup? Is it their necessity? Need for money? Status? On-the-job self-actualisation? Desire to excel and achieve? Fear of losing the job? Is the business player a self-challenger or is running out of fear? I don't know your experience, but I find most of us are doing what we are doing because we have nothing better to do. Frankly I do not regard fear as a motivator. It may get work done, but for me it is not a motivator. For me, motivation has to be a self-generated desire to achieve; an adventurous, joyful, exploratory happy journey. I do not know if I have been able to communicate my thoughts or not."

He went on to elaborate, "In almost every industry, information and communication technology is transforming more and more jobs that are defined by targets and routine processes. With my limited experience in that industry, even in the high-profile investment banking industry, computer-guided financial statements are near decision-option ready. I may be wrong, but what is left is administration and sales — routine processes and targets. Not very mind challenging assignments."

After some elaborations of his concepts, he went on to say, "In response to the economic imperatives of their global value chains, the job profiles in different localities are changing, often creating a chasm between aspirations and reality. Large corporations, by nature have to be impersonal systems led with clearly-stated and input/output-defined jobs, and a little transparency. But, appointment columns in newspapers are full of job profiles that do not exist anywhere in the business arena. Thus new recruits often start with disappointment. Motivating disillusioned team players over a long period would be a challenge for future managers."

"Exploring ways to be more efficient and effective in the existing business would continue to be a challenge. Finding new ways to enhance value for customers, by reducing cost or adding new service features to enhance customer satisfaction would continue to be a challenge in a competitive market. That is why we keep hearing about the critical importance of ideas. Ideas for small improvements in services, as in kaizen approach to enhance happiness of customers," said a lady in a global health care organisation.

After a pause she continued, "I feel we should make clear distinctions between ideas and innovations. From my perspective, ideas are about improving existing value chains and innovations are for a new set of customers, with new business models and new value chains. Developing a new customer is much more risky and at least five times more expensive. We need to be simultaneously 'kaizenists' as well as 'innovationists' to meet the challenges of developing our managerial talents in the shortest possible time. Also, we need to be information and communication technology savvy."

"Aligning corporate structures, processes and systems to the new global business economic realities, would be a critical challenge for corporate leaders. In the fast-changing global business environment, to play the global business game effectively, corporations would need to constantly align their corporate economic equations with those of the global supply chain imperatives," said an international business consultant. After some elaborations he went on to say, "But all this requires appropriate talent. Do we have the required managerial resources to understand and meet the evolving challenges? I feel the real challenge is to develop appropriate managerial skills." After further discussion he went on to say, "I feel our present management education system does not provide the required sense of real change that is taking place in the domestic and global business arenas. The management education has been too structured for too long; it has aged. We are in need of a status-quo shift. The textbooks provided, the case studies used and the pedagogies adopted by management schools are not in tune with the current requirements of the business arena. B-schools are long on jargons, skills and styles but short on real substance. B-school 'attitude' is a much discussed topic in the corporate world. I very strongly feel we need to face the evolving challenges with new and appropriate perspectives. Do the management school faculty members have the required time, data, contextual information and understanding of case studies used by them in classrooms? Are they providing appropriate understanding and insights of the business issues involved? Are the case studies appropriate and relevant to the prevailing business realities? What is the definition of a good or appropriate case study? How should it be used? All business is situational. What is the lifecycle of a case study? With what covets? Does the faculty have the required training to handle case studies? How much time is allocated to understanding and defining the problems, formulating appropriate questions and reasoning the relevance and context of case studies used? Does the management faculty have the required domain knowledge? These and many more such questions have come to my mind as you asked me about the challenges and opportunities for the business players in the evolving global business arena." He concluded with the observation, "Inappropriate knowledge bases, skill sets and mindsets can often do more damage than good to business operations. Besides the skills to acquire data and information, we need knowledge and wisdom to use them appropriately."

"The challenge is to make optimal use of information and knowledge resources available to corporations both internally as well as from outside sources and to identify sustainable growth options for corporations and transform them into gainful business processes," said a senior manager, head of the strategy group in a large organisation. After some elaborations he went on to say, "Today, corporations are faced with many new forms of challenges and hazards. As corporations adopt more and more computer-dependent infrastructure they are faced with sophisticated cyber hacking from amateur internet warriors as well as global competitors. Corporate cyberwars are a reality. Cyber warfare would be a critical component of future commercial wars. It may be possible to give a crippling blow to an identified competitor through the global cyberspace. One often hears of hackers breaking into high-security networks. Thus, the corporations have to be ready for the new challenges to their security and strategic planning from the cyber warriors."

"There is no dearth of opportunities in any area of business, social and economic or technology, or any other area for that matter. The challenge is in clearly defining one's target. You will be surprised to know how few, in fact very few, post graduate students really know what they want when they join MBA programmes. Many finish the MBA programmes without knowing what they really want to do. They just pick up jobs from the options that come in their way. The interest, enthusiasm, and the desire to excel have to be imposed on by corporations. Creating enthusiastic corporate teams would be a major challenge for managers," said the vice-president of human resources of a large organisation.

"I have heard speakers and executives at many seminars discuss their job profiles with unenthusiastic feelings. They often term their jobs as repetitive and unchallenging. It is also often said that technology and innovative softwares instead of making their jobs more challenging and interesting are making most jobs mundane and repetitive. They also observe that in most large transnational organisations, major decisions are taken at their global corporate offices. All they are left to do is to implement decisions. All they end up getting are targets, time frames and some occasional pep talks. In corporate meetings they often ask, where is the challenge in the global arena?" said a senior human resource consultant.

After elaboration on some points he went on to say, "The problem is a misfit or disconnect between the job and the executive. It is a serious lacuna in our business education. Students acquire skill sets without knowing what job they want to do. Education and management institutes provide them with a fixed set of inputs. The current rote teaching and faculty evaluation by students leads to status quo rather than promote change and experimentation. Discussions of some high profile case studies in class give them illusions of corporate heroes. They visualise the glamour side of business like decisions being made on the golf course or at night clubs. They see the glamour side of catwalks and not the details and efforts that go into making the show. They enter the business world with illusions and not with a sense of reality."

After another diversion on related topics, he went on to say, "Every job has its own set of challenges. Each requires specific skills. One may be over qualified for a job. If the job specifications and the required skill sets, both hard and soft, do not match with those of the selected candidate, one is bound to have a sense of frustration."

Elaborating on some alternate solutions, he went on to say, "Our education system must be realistic. With innovative use of various technologies, corporations are taking a global view of their business economics and value chains. The global job scenario is in a flux. The knowledge bases, skill sets and mindsets or attitude that national corporations require are different from those required in jobs of MNCs operating in India. Because of mismatches between the expectations from the job and jobs-on-offer, and the skill sets which the candidates bring with them and those that are required, there are lots of unnecessary costs and wastage of voluble corporate resources. I feel, educational institutes and B-schools need to take a fresh look at their curriculum and pedagogies. Also, I feel there is an urgent need for an open forum dialogue between corporations and B-schools, in designing their graduate and executive training programmes."

"I feel B-schools need a system where change is an integral part of the learning process. One should be able to feel and experience the change. The faculty is not evaluated by the students on the basis of how they meet the traditional norms but how they promote original thinking in students.

It is difficult to break old habits. Students used to rote learning will not like it. I feel the purpose of education should not be a test ability of students to take information, store it and reproduce it in an examination — like a computer hard disk. Frankly, while a student of a much respected B-school I felt I was expected to behave like a computer hard disk. Personally, I did not like it," said a senior lady executive in the health care industry.

"A nation is as good as its people. To be good or productive and a value-adding citizen, one does not have to be necessarily educated, but education helps. Appropriate education is critical to make optimal use of human resources. As the global industrial scenario is going through rapid changes, I feel it is time that we take a futuristic view of education. Critically assess use of information and communication technology as well as global connectivity in the education process. For investments in education to yield appropriate returns, we need to have a fairly realistic view of the business world and its emerging job profiles. Depending on their global business options, MNC often make sudden shifts in their job locations to different parts of the world. Human resource development which is often referred to as talent-development operations, need to be job focused. Mismatch between talent development and job requirements creates wastage of human resources and growth opportunities. I feel we need to take a critical look at our education and talent development systems," said a recently retired senior executive of a multinational organisation.

"I feel our education system should be such that each one can optimise one's potential and pursue activity areas of their own interest. The system should generate enthusiasm to explore and excel in their areas of interest. In a large country like ours, with unlimited growth potentials in almost every area of economic and social activity, I feel each individual should be able to explore and find their pursuit in life that would give them happiness and growth," said a senior lady executive in the education administration.

After some discussions, on related topics she went on to elaborate, "We need an education system that makes people self-starters. With the availability of Internet in most parts of the country, we need to bridge the gap between rural and urban learning opportunities. We need to inculcate the self-motivated and determined learning spirit of Eaklavya. Today, in the entrepreneurial market economy, individuals are themselves responsible for development of their own careers. Thus, our education system should lay emphasis on self-reliance and the entrepreneurship spirit. The challenge for corporations is to identify and develop competent and proactive business leaders."

With the various perspectives of challenges and opportunities, the obvious question that often cropped up was about the alternate response options and road maps that may be appropriate and effective to cope with the challenges and also help transform opportunities into gainful ventures. Thus began the search for some solutions.

5

Response Options

"Education, more education and more appropriate education is what we need to meet the future challenges of competitive development. In the current hypercompetitive knowledge era, illiteracy is a deadly weakness. Also as is often said, little knowledge is a dangerous thing and can be very dangerous in the current fast-changing business environment. In the evolving knowledge economy, it is meaningless to talk about national demographic advantages or disadvantages without taking into account the useful talent and education levels of the population. Education is the principle mover of society. Education energises human resources. Without appropriate education our national growth would not be sustainable. And, like everything else, there is a right kind of education and a wrong kind of education. It all depends on our objectives and priorities and our national mission; after all education is about the future, about things happening around us. We need education to gain respect for ourselves in our own eyes. Knowledge is the most critical success factor today and for the future. Education empowers people to enhance their chances to live their lives the way they want to. The effective response would have to come from appropriate education. Time to invest in education is now. To come out as winners, our response must match the global challenges. By response I mean developing our capacities, capabilities and competencies to meet the challenges and take advantage of the opportunities before us, within the country and abroad," said a senior lady CEO in the publishing industry.

After some discussions, she concluded, "Education is critical to meet requirements of the evolving knowledge era. India has the potential to be a major global learning centre. For a nation, it is never too early to invest in education. Education is the prime mover of societies. I feel we should aspire to be a global *gurukul.*"

Speaking on similar lines a CEO of an NGO said, "Optimal use of resources is one of the main objectives of any economic system. Education is the prime mover of human resources. Appropriate education that promotes self-reliance and entrepreneurial spirit is the most desired social need. I feel employment levels are major indicators of economic happiness of a society. Quality and quantity of employment is a major concern of social scientists. Thus the critical role of education cannot be overstated in the evolving information and knowledge era." After some elaborations he summed up, "This is an era of *Lakshmi* following *Saraswati.* Money and prosperity will follow education."

"Brainpower is the mother of all powers. Brainpower is the basis of industrial power and competitiveness. Brainpower is the basis of agricultural power. Brainpower is the basis of military power. Brainpower is the basis of national self-confidence. What we need is to develop our national brainpower base, by appropriate universal education. We need to see the vital importance of appropriate primary, secondary, vocational and tertiary education for all," said a retired army officer.

After some elaborations he continued and said, "In the rapidly evolving knowledge era, the lifecycle of knowledge is reducing fast. The rate of knowledge obsolesce is increasing. One has to constantly update and upgrade one's brainpower, knowledge and intellectual capital. As I see it, brainpower is the ability to store useful information; knowledge is the ability to clearly define problems; and intellectual capital is the ability to implement solutions." He concluded with the observation, "I strongly believe that today it is no longer survival of the fittest but survival of the wisest — one who can recognize opportunity and transform it into a profitable working proposition."

"Management, more effective management and still more effective management, is what we need to meet the needs of industry, agriculture and aspirations of our citizens. Our natural resources are depleting fast and the expectations of consumers and citizens are rising. Unless we start managing every aspect of our lives — as individuals, families, society, agriculturists, politicians, business operators and environmentalists, we may soon be in an unprecedented crisis. We need to develop our capabilities and competencies to sustain our development and growth momentum. With a large population and limited resources, we have to learn to make optimal use of our resources. We need to develop and share managerial perspective with people in all walks of life." After sharing some of her observations and concerns, a senior lady executive of a rural development organisation continued, "Management should be taught and practiced as a social science or an article-of-faith. Just look around and see how much inefficiency and wastage there is all around us; wastage that can be easily avoided is happening all around us. To take advantage of the global opportunities around us, we need to learn to manage our available resources effectively. The race for global resources is already on. Every citizen has a role in national management. To be counted as good global citizens and a nation of responsible citizens we need to manage our resources effectively. Issues such as air and water pollution as well as climate change affect us all."

Commenting on the subject of human resource development, a senior management consultant observed, "It is a well-established fact that education is the key to economic development. Imperatives of appropriate situation-specific management education cannot be overstated, especially in the evolving, dynamic, increasingly competitive, rapidly globalising as well as changing social and economic environment."

After some digressions on geo-political issues, he went on to say, "Globalisation is another name for economic warfare. Economic wars are fought with economic resources and for economic resources. Talent and customers are also resources; two sides of the human being. We need to make the best use of available resources. Human capital is the most critical asset. Currently that is our strongest as well as the weakest link. The global economic system is in the fast-forward mode. The more powerful and energetic transnational corporations are striving to capture entire sectors of the global market that encompasses more than just the individual products or services."

Elaborating on the subject he said, "We cannot hide away from these realities. Today there is competition between nations, corporations, states, even between cities, towns and individuals in the same family. There is competition between political parties and state bureaucracies. Competition is a mind game. We need world-class education to be world-class competitors. Education helps in gaining an advantageous position in any form of competition. Taking into account that all business is local, to be effective, management education must provide an effectual local-global perspective." After a thoughtful pause he said, "I wonder, whether we have an apt word or expression for *competition* in our national languages. At times I feel competition or the real competitive spirit is not a part of our national culture or national ethos."

Expressing her views on the critical role of human resource development in social and national development, a vice-president of human resource management of a large multinational organisation said, "I think we have a lot to learn from the former Chinese leader Deng Xiaoping who would say that it did not matter whether a cat was black or white, as long as it caught mice. Our main focus should be to develop our human resources. We need to develop our human resources as a top priority. As we delay, we broaden our problem. An untrained or illiterate person tends to become a lifelong liability. I think we lack a realistic management perspective of our national human resources. Because of our neglect, we are creating large pools of avoidable future human liabilities, perhaps very sensitive social land mines."

Elaborating on similar lines an entrepreneur owner of a midsize business unit said, "I am a Tamil Brahmin; I attended an Irish Catholic School and was taught by a Muslim teacher; I am grateful to them all." He went on to say, "We need to be openminded to learn from any source we can. A resourceful human life, I feel, is wasted without education. Also the community and the nation miss out on the creativity because of the lack of an educated mind. We must remove all barriers to learning within a broad national education policy framework. I feel we should try and make India a global learning centre in every area of learning. And use information and communication technologies in creating national and global-learning alliances."

Expressing her views on the subject a lady social worker commented, "Human resource is a very sensitive and perishable resource. We need to initiate its development at the right time in the right direction to be economically useful. Each day lost means an opportunity gone forever. Today, we have the highest number of illiterates in the world. We are the most illiterate nation on earth which is the basic cause of our national guilt, shame, anger and resentment. We need to use all possible means to transform our young illiterate population into our potential talent bank, and shape them into significant individuals and long-term value-generating assets to the nation. An illiterate person is almost a wasted human resource, perhaps forever." She concluded with an observation, "As citizens of a democracy, I feel we are all responsible for the current state of affairs. We are all in need of management education. At least common sense of managing as well as developing our most valuable perishable human resources, which otherwise would turn into a massive social liability."

"Global competition has as much to do with the quality of our government (our governance of national institutions) as it has to do with the efficiency of our corporations. It all boils down to the quality of our general education, our information base, our knowledge, our ability to dream, our ability to aspire, our desire to do better and our can-do attitude," said a retired chief executive of a public sector unit.

"We need to transform our cost advantage into knowledge and intellectual capital advantage. Cost (or poverty) cannot remain a competitive advantage for long. Education will help us improve our productivity and enlarge our knowledge base. Provide a base for a future-sustainable competitive advantage," said a lady business executive. After some discussions on various topics, she went on to say, "Without the proper education of our citizens, can we walk on the global footpaths holding our heads high? As a nation, we do have a lot to be proud of but we also have a lot to be ashamed of. I think we need to ask ourselves — are we a part of a global problem or an active ingredient in contributing to global solutions? Are we a factor in enhancing human dignity or reducing human dignity?"

"Sustainable competitive advantages in the global business arena cannot be based on cost advantage alone. It also requires individual and corporate brainpower, corporate intellectual capital, customer relationship management, and the ability to innovate and transform innovations into competitive business advantages successfully," said a business consultant. After some discussions she went on to say, "Change is never easy, particularly when it involves complex cross-cultural and transnational issues as well as diverse interests."

When asked to give their views on alternatives approaches to human development a CMD of a medium size industrial unit said, "We must be clear in our objectives. Our main national concern should be to provide appropriate education to as many children and adults as we can, and as fast as we can. The key word is appropriate. We need to make full use of available information and communication technology options. Making use of technology, many business organisations are reaching rural areas, even remote areas, and integrating them into their marketing frameworks effectively."

He went on to say, "Frankly I do not think we suffer from a lack of resources. If anything, we suffer from our own individual managerial short-sightedness and mental blocks. As a nation, we have a learning culture. Educated people have always been respected in India. Imparting education, as a social activity, has also been well thought of. We would do well to make education a national priority with active participation of the general public, especially youth, in the campaigns such as: each-one-teach-one or share-your-learning. I feel it should be a national youth led movement with active participation of schools and corporations, the media, advertising and communication industry as well as the film industry, and organisations such as the Federation of Indian Chambers of Commerce and Industry (FICCI) and the Confederation of Indian Industry (CII)."

"A nation is as good as its human resources. Appropriate education is essential to transform human resource into progressive high value-adding citizens," were the thoughts of a committed lady social worker from rural India. She went on to say, "India should not even think of calling herself an economic superpower with its current deceitful definition of literacy and miserably low levels of literacy. Notwithstanding all the extensive rhetoric about 'Shining

India,' 'Incredible India' or a 'Trillion-Dollar Economy,' we need moral courage to be honest about our social realities. Like ostriches, we should not wish them away. Today, a large majority of our population is mired in abject conditions. A backlash of social divide may be brutal for us all. We should either try and manage it now or be ready to get minced by it later."

She also went on to say, "People like you and I, represent less than one percent of India. And, how secure and comfortable are we in absolute or relative terms? Just think about it and try to put it in the national perspective. In cities, individual-driven private cars are becoming bigger and multiplying while public transport facilities are becoming more and more inefficient, ineffective as well as less and less affordable for the average citizen. The economic and social gaps are increasing. Frankly, I find it a scary scenario. The response has to be realistic with socio-economic focus."

"There is a lot of talk about positioning India in the global arena. What is it that stands between India and its rightful place in the global arena? As far as I can see, it is the lack of imagination and our courage to be Indians. Notwithstanding all the diversity, the spirit of India has to be there. We have to respect ourselves before we expect others to respect us. It is important to have an aspiration for growth because it recharges and focuses the national mind. It is time to talk of opportunities and challenges. It is an era of responsibility, integrity and accountability for every citizen. Only appropriate education can empower citizens," said a lady university teacher. After some discussions she went on to say, "History is important, but I feel, we must not let our history obstruct our growth and vision of the future. We need to build on our history. Our future should be better than our past."

Commenting on the theme of human resource development, a middle-aged non-resident Indian visiting India said, "I feel there are a large number of Indians in the global Indian Diaspora, looking for a cause to do their bit for their communities and country and education would be very close to their heart."

He went on to elaborate, "Next year should be declared as the year for primary education — eradication of illiteracy in a specified age group. NGOs in different parts of India committed to education, should contact NRIs as a group as well as individuals with their action plans. Using global cyberlinks, contextual credible models should be mutually worked out. It could be a contribution for the creation of an additional classroom in an existing school or the contribution for a mid-day meal fund, to create a new school, to adopt a school, to adopt a student, a long-term scholarship scheme, or for any other mutually agreed upon primary education promotion plan. It should be real action and actual performance oriented and a participative build-and-operate plan. Every interested person should be able to participate according to one's desire."

Suggesting an overall framework he said, "The government, local communities and *Panchayats* in rural areas should be encouraged to be active partners. Government support is essential in providing a clearly defined broad education policy where public-private partnerships (PPP), NRI/NGO-*Panchayat* partnerships (N2P2), NRI/NGO partnerships (N2P) or any other form of cooperative venture in this area should be able to operate within the specified education policy framework. Internet and information technology enabled services (ITeS) should be extensively used for this venture."

Concluding his observations he said, "I am not an information technology (IT) person, but I feel we should be able to come up with a helpful cost effective and a user friendly IT-enabled service based primary education system, for different remote regions of India — an operational framework based on our national needs and proven strengths."

Expressing his concerns on the impact of globalisation, a senior executive in international business said, "I feel that while market economies have certain advantages, there are also some disadvantages in market-oriented systems. One should not underestimate the linkages between employment, economic nationalism and country's political aspirations. It is a well-known fact that lobbies and political leverages are used by transnational corporations to pry open national markets. Also, in many cases new sophisticated business strategies are being used in place of old crude military options. Currently, it is an era of global business warfare and market conquests. Technology and money power are having a field day on the world business scene."

After elaboration further on some of the points he went on to say, "Capitalism and market economy are games of self-interest. Market forces are independent of moral values. While encouraging corporations to play their business game, protecting self-interest are the responsibilities of individuals, societies and nations. Also, the winning edge of the transnational corporations often lies in the weakness of institutions, laws, systems and governance of many countries."

After elaborating on some of his observations he went on to say, "To respond to the evolving global challenges and opportunities in a systematic manner, we need to have a national debate on our national mission or a vision of ourselves as a nation in the geo-political arena. Appropriate education, more so technical and management education, would be a critical success factor in realising our aims and ambitions in the global arena."

After sharing some of his personal experiences in international business transactions, he went on to conclude, "Today, India sparkles with entrepreneurial and commercial verve. However, globally it is a relatively minor player on the international economic scene. Its international business aggregates to about one percent of the global transactions.

Its economic standing in the comity of nations, so far, does not befit its size, population or domestic resource potential. A lot remains to be done, if India is to play a meaningful role on the world economic scene."

"I may sound a bit old fashioned and offbeat, but frankly I feel India's response to globalisation should be based on our own historical strengths. We have done a lot of aping of the West. Please do not misunderstand me; I am not against learning from the West or any other source. I have also had part of my education in the West. I have an open mind and believe in learning from every one. But, I feel India needs Indian solutions."

After explaining some of his thoughts, he went on to say, "We need to understand the real causes of our social and economic problems. We need to understand our social, economic and political problems from our own historic perspective. We need to debate among ourselves. Why have we neglected our own regional languages as a medium of education? Why can management not be taught in local languages in the local context? Management is needed everywhere in every activity. Our rural areas also need modern management concepts in their local contexts."

Sharing her views on the same topic the lady CEO of an NGO said, "Even today, after more than sixty years of independence, we don't have management education books written by our own authors. Why? Why do we not have management books written in our own official languages, dealing with our own social, economic and business problems? Why? Why are management subjects not being taught in our own languages? Don't we need management in rural areas? Is management only needed in selling junk food, soaps and credit cards? Where have we gone wrong? We are only adding to our social divisions. We are creating more and more social and economic castes. We need more and more microfinance and micro-entrepreneurship ventures to break through the massive vicious cycle of poverty."

After elaborating on some of her points she went on to explain, "For too long we have had urban-centric focus. Urban VIP cult seems to dominate our thinking. I feel we still suffer from the hangover of the British *babu raj*. We are yet to wake up to our real Indian realities — urban and especially rural. Our IAS is still in the shadows of ICS. Remote rural India is an interesting subject to be discussed in air-conditioned urban halls. Even the Lok Sabha politicians come to seek votes from the illiterate, poor and hungry, moving on especially sanitised roads and in air-conditioned cars. To answer your question, as a response to globalisation, I feel we need to make every citizen aware of his and her rights as well as obligations to improve conditions around them as well as for us all. We need management education for every citizen. I feel it should be an integral part of our school education curriculum," she concluded with a feeling of concern.

Speaking on similar lines a CEO of a rural bank said, "Why is management education considered such an elite study? Management is just a process of using common sense in our daily activities, in family matters or on the job. During my long career, I have managed various financial institutions of different sizes; I find it has been just a matter of understanding the procedures and using common sense in selecting the options. I have also won awards for innovation, which in fact was just a simple observation which facilitated some banking services for our customers."

After sharing some of his experiences he went on to say, "Management is a much over-hyped term. Why is it thought of as an elite subject I fail to understand. Graduates of B-schools have to do a lot of unlearning and re-learning before they become effective executives. After joining banks and other financial institutions, many of them feel frustrated by its simplicity. I feel business schools create false hyped-up images in their minds. May be this is done to strengthen their brand and create justification for their charging high fees. In a way I feel this is a disservice to the future managers and society. I feel management is a simple common sense activity and it should be taught in a simple, interesting and creative way as a game to improve customer service. What is so elite about management education, I really do not understand."

After elaborating on some of the above points he went on to say, "To meet the challenges of globalisation, I feel we should make management a common subject for all students. We need to be aware of the virtues of good management at all levels of society. We need managerial alertness for managing our local resources more productively and in improving our local management processes."

"To take advantage of the opportunities provided by globalisation, I feel we should try to create world-class clusters of education for different disciplines. These clusters should have global participation and global video-conferencing linkages. Different clusters may be created for general purpose education and for those offering specialisations. These must have global-research orientation also. This would help India become a global learning hub," said the retired principal of a nationally renowned public school.

Speaking on similar lines a medical doctor said, "We need to create world-class global health care clusters with extensive facilities for training and research. These should be technologically integrated and need based to serve even the remotest areas."

Providing an industry perspective on the above lines a senior business consultant said, "We need to create industry-specific clusters to make India a critical value-adding link in the global value chain of different industries. These clusters by necessity have to have a collaborative approach. Participants would have to include industry members, consultants, technology institutes, business schools and research organisations. We will need to have a global perspective and a futuristic outlook. Perhaps, to be more effective, the clusters could be globally networked industry-technology-research-academia clusters. Competition after all is a game of human resource productivity."

After some discussions on related topics he went on to say, "We need to create and encourage global links at all levels — people-to-people, industry-to-industry and nation-to-nation. I feel industry associations need to become proactive in this."

After explaining some of his concepts he went on to say, "In the global arena, India needs to differentiate itself on the basis of its democracy, diversity and divinity. For long, we have been learners and exporters of spirituality. At the same time we need to set our house in order and minimise disparity in our society."

Providing an Indian-Ocean perspective, a deep seabed mining expert said, "We have a large coastline. Indian Ocean is the only ocean named after a country. I feel it offers us a number of options for growth. Besides development of various ocean-based industries, we can develop the Indian Ocean into an ocean of oceanic sports. We can think of exploring possibilities of creating floating universities or business schools that touch and study different coastal cities around the Indian Ocean during their educational tenures. This may also be a collaborative venture with other Indian Ocean rim countries. Many other collaborative ventures can be innovatively worked out for mutual gains."

"We need to develop a framework for Indian-global corporate citizenship. As Indian corporations go abroad, they must do so with Indian values of mutual respect and sharing, with the spirit of *vasudeva kutumbhkam* (world is a family), notwithstanding the prevailing dysfunctions in the global village. Indian corporations should try to be model global-corporate citizens with global human values. Being a good corporate citizen is good for business also," said a senior executive of a business association.

A senior executive of an advertising company observed, "There has been a lot of talk about brand India. I feel to be meaningful a brand has to be customer and objective specific. For appropriate and effective brand India, I feel it would be advantageous for us to segment our global relations into at least four broad distinct segments — government, industry, tourism and education. Each of these should evolve their own objective and customer specific global brand-building strategies." After some elaborations, he concluded with the statement, "Each country must work out its own priorities and plans for its future positioning in the global arena."

Our initial efforts to gain some understanding of the perceived responses to emerging challenges provided us with reactions in indicative and general terms. They provided us rather blurred images and a hazy vision. In continuation of our learning efforts, we made repeated efforts to gain insights by being more specific in terms of business models and associated job profiles, which are likely to emerge in the global business arena. At times, the discussions trespassed on to topics and subjects such as corporate and organisational behaviour, structures and governance norms, as well as the required knowledge bases, skill sets and mindsets for the evolving global organisations.

We tried to focus on gaining insights of evolving global business models and job profiles. The subject became more relevant with the turmoil in the global 'casino' financial markets as well as the real economic arenas.

6

Emerging Global Business Models and Job Profiles

"Transformation, more transformation and still more future-focused transformation. To cope with the fast-changing business environment, corporate designs and structures are going through continuous transformation. Economics of the corporate global value chains are shifting all the time. As we are basically in the manufacturing operations, corporate value chain may be seen as a chain of transformational activities linked by transactional activities with a consumer focus. New sourcing and outsourcing options along with technological developments often make it mandatory to transform corporate systems and relocate some of its business processes. Emergence of new technologies and demographic profile shifts as well as population shifts, impact corporate structures and their business models. Increasing competitive pressures result in corporate, processes, business partners and supply chain fragmentations. Work begins to flow to where it is done best and most economically. Thus new business models and corporate structures are evolving all the time within the framework of global corporate strategic thinking and plans. We are always on the lookout for more economical production bases as well as lucrative markets. It may not be wrong to say that we are in a perpetual search for dynamic equilibrium," said the senior vice-president of a multinational corporation.

"I like to look at corporations as information and knowledge conglomerates — a conglomerate of diverse domain knowledge bases and skill sets. Knowledge is the lifeblood or lifeline of most, if not all, business organisations. However, knowledge to be useful has to be managed appropriately and strategically. Also, to be useful, knowledge has to be target focused. For a business the ultimate target is customer. Knowledge, as I see it, is the ability to identify as well as envision opportunities to add value for current or new set of customers in a fast-changing business environment. Here, knowledge may also be seen as a sum total of customer insights. It is also the ability to design a workable road map to them," said a senior executive in a multinational organisation.

After some elaborations, he went on to say, "As the global opportunities expand, corporations are looking for appropriate locations to nurture and expand their knowledge bases as well as skill sets. Effective use of ITeS provides a reliable means for economic global connectivity and delivery of services. Visa or no visa, for all practical purposes, human capital is globally portable today, even when different parts of the world speak different business languages. Business fads, fashions and jargons keep changing. During my interactions in different countries, I found that even the concept and word strategy has a different meaning in different parts of the world. Thus, corporate global value chain and global structure goes through business partners and local customer-focused morphing. Global connectivity helps in optimising global value chains. Many low productivity and performance issues can be traced back to poor and inappropriate organisation designs and business models. This is where one gets to display his or her skills in opportunity identification, innovation and change management; attracting, delighting and retaining diverse cross-cultural customers."

"Frankly, I do not see any trends. To me it seems each industry is unique and reacting differently to globalisation, with its own economic considerations. Each industry is morphing in its own unique way. Each corporation in each industry has its own history, business leadership thinking, business culture, business processes, business alliances, networks and partners. Each competitive business unit is a distinct customer-focused efficiency-led organisation. Like individuals each corporation has its own short-term and long-term perspectives. Each CEO reacts to market challenges and opportunities differently. Each company has its own selected customer segments in different parts of the world, to which it is catering in its own unique way as effectively as it can. Even close competitors, when examined closely, are very different in their internal structures, business processes and external relations. Each corporation embroiders its own pattern on the global fabric," said a senior lady executive of a transnational corporation.

After explaining some of her observations, she summed up thus: "I feel, like individuals, each corporation is evolving differently in the global arena. Each executive and each corporation has its own way of listening to customers and learning from its markets. I would not like to generalise or see any trend. In our own case, even internally our different divisions often react very differently to the same global happenings. Also, to succeed, we have to do something different or something differently, while remaining customer focused. It is the need for effective focus on different sets of customers in different countries that determines our corporate architecture. Customer focus with a competitive response is our corporate objective. Our business model is based on our corporate objectives."

"While thinking of evolving business models, I think we need to keep in mind that corporations respond differently to their prevailing and expected business environment. In the competitive global business arena, local-global morphing of customers is taking place at different speeds and in a variety of patterns in different markets. Each organisation designs its own response strategies. One can see the matrix and dynamics of localisation of global products as well as globalisation of local products. In the global arena, besides various other issues, all corporations have to cope with issues of fostering trust, meet the challenges of cultural cross-currents and optimise their centralisation-decentralisation strategic options. Again, we must remember that, like individuals, corporations have their own mindsets, emotions and conventions," said a senior business consultant.

After some discussions, he concluded with the following observations: "Talent, technology and business topography determine the corporate structures and business models. Also, it is important to remember that it is not the most intelligent or the strongest that survive and grow in a competitive environment but the one most responsive to change; one who can perceive growth opportunities in change."

"Globalisation brings to the table whole new sets of options and opportunities. Every industry offers unique opportunities to learn, options to explore and challenges to launch a whole new set of products and services with new business models. Information technology and global connectivity provides new local and global support systems. Kaizen and innovation have to be a way of life in the business organisation; an integral continuous process as well as a part of the corporate culture," said the CEO of a medium size fashion export organisation. After some elaborations she said, "I feel, even in the well developed so-called global markets, consumers seem to be in search of their own identity in their own unique way. We just have to look, listen and try to understand the human consumer behind the plastic credit card. Frankly, I have not seen a flat market. At times it seems that localisation is increasing much faster than globalisation. Also, local-global-mix priorities keep changing. For survival and growth, keeping in mind the dynamics of lingual, cultural and income diversities, we not only need new thinking with regards to products and services but also new business models to meet the expectations of consumers and business partners. Each company has to define, demarcate and cut its own market slice from the global cake."

"I feel the future global business models will be cost and customer centric. Talent and technology would provide the global sinews between resources and customers. Knowledge will be the blood that will flow through the whole corporate nervous system. Corporations will take on most cost-effective and customer-centric structures. To minimise internal operational constraints, the corporate architecture and operational framework would have a judicious real-virtual mix. Information technology would play a critical role. We have to critically examine the required role of technology along with human personality, emotions, attitudes, skill sets and knowledge bases. Some jobs will be technology led, some skills led, some personality led and some knowledge led. A corporation will have a dynamic mix of all these. The nature of human talent requirements will keep changing," said a senior executive of an information technology organisation.

After some elaborations of his concepts he went on to say, "Customer-centric innovation would be the main objective of corporations. Be it ideas for blue ocean strategies or suggestions for kaizen; be it for improvements in the business process or add value to products, innovations would be needed to sustain growth in the competitive environment. To take on broad innovative ideas from different sections of employees from different parts of the world, corporations would have to adopt cross-cultural global communication networks." He concluded with the observation, "The challenge would be to create a business model that is proactive, customer knowledge focused, flexible and is efficient in learning, so that new knowledge can easily be embedded in the business processes and systems or it easily transforms knowledge into corporate intellectual capital or operational reality."

"In the multicultural fast-changing global business arena, corporations will have to learn the skills and the art of Parkour. I see it as a target-focused, mind-body activity. The important thing to know about Parkour is that it is not about crossing obstacles. It is about getting from point A to point B, as fast as one can, by making use of whatever is in one's path as support or help. It requires fast, situation specific, innovative, target-focused thinking. It would require business players to think like *traceurs* or *traceuses*," said a senior executive in the global supply operations. After some elaborations he went on to say, "As it is the global business arena, each obstacle a *traceur* faces, presents unique challenges, opportunities and advantages. Each challenge calls for a unique approach. The technique that works in one situation may or may not work in another. That is what has been my own experience in the global business game."

"I am not sure if any single business model will be or can be suitable for all industries or all corporations. Whatever the model, in the global business arena, each global player to remain competitive and grow will need global level operational competencies. These will depend on global sourcing of talents and technologies. However, the real challenge would be to relate global talent, technologies and systems to local customers. All customers are local and operate in local environments. Thus, at the end of the day, the management of global-local dynamics would determine success of business models, an effective mix of global-local or national-international work culture," said a senior executive in international banking.

"Notwithstanding all the hype about cost advantages, I feel, we have to realise that the global business world is not led by cost alone. I do realise that cost is a critical factor in business operations. But, repetitively speaking of cost as a competitive advantage, I often feel we are trying to make virtue out of our poverty." After elaborating his point, this senior executive of an advertising agency went on to say, "Besides cost, the competitive advantages also originate from skills, productivity, customer relations, development of corporate as well as product and service brands, building up know-how and fostering innovations."

Elaborating further on global competition, he said, "We need to critically analyse the situation and ask — have we been paying too much respect to the strengths of our international competitors? Corporations using their advertising and communication strategies often create a mental trap for consumers and competitors. I feel we also need to do a target specific, objective and critical analysis of our real strengths and weaknesses in commercial, emotional as well as intellectual areas. Consumers, do respond to values." He concluded with the observation: "We need to be pragmatic. I feel values are situation specific, not absolute and static."

"The future business model for a corporation will depend on many factors. Besides its business history and culture, products and service range, business processes and business policy frame work, its business model will depend on how it wants to globalise its operations; the road map for the global arena it has created for itself. The appropriateness of its business model will depend on its capacity as well as readiness for internationalisation, its capacity to appreciate and absorb foreign business cultures, and its approach to gain understanding of foreign customers. Global business is a risky game. One has to be business as well as cross-cultural savvy. The global business arena is full of sick and injured corporations as well as of corporate graves," said a CEO from the international hospitality industry. After elaborating on some of his observations, he went on to say, "The global business arena is full of paradoxes and surprises. One needs an open and learning mind. One would have to be flexible and innovative in designing an appropriate business model." He concluded with the observation: "I like to see large transnational corporations as global business-oriented communities."

"I like to think of a company as a collection of diverse energies — mental, emotional, spiritual and physical. Corporations may be seen as energy flow processes. Their competitiveness depends on the sum total and effective use of these energies. Besides various other forms, corporations need energies to visualise and plan, energies to implement, and energies to do-as-told. Depending on their business objectives and roadmaps, corporations have to estimate their energy needs and develop their individual energy score card. For optimal results, each energy base has to be nurtured individually, appropriately and synergistically. Each organisation is constantly in search of ways to enhance quality and quantity of its energy levels. Corporate energy may also be seen as the sum total of the energy of its individual employees. Technology, as I see it, is an energy support system. Managements need to identify causes for energy depleting behaviour of their employees. A good and effective corporate system energises and synergises the individual energies. For this to happen, as far as possible, the corporate system has to be friction free. I like to call it corporate energy optimising model," said a senior management consultant.

After some elaborations he went on to say, "Some corporations creatively use information technology and the Internet to connect and enhance energy and corporate intellectual levels. For example, to interactively synergise global individual energies, global corporate blogs constitute an integral part of business models."

After explaining some of his concepts he said, "I feel the corporate growth should be led by the direction and intensity of corporate energy flows. Corporate management has to be sensitive to the level and flow of global cross-cultural corporate energy." After some discussions he said, "Under this model, for optimal corporate energy use, global corporations would be led by individual local units. Energy bases are local, energy flows may be global."

"Today in business, innovation does not mean just a new product or a service for a different set of customers. I feel, it means, anything that adds value for consumers qualifies as innovation. As I see it, any improvement in sourcing, processing, distribution or retailing that provides a competitive edge would qualify as innovation. A reduction in transaction cost or minimising wastages in different business processes would also be innovation. Be it in the domestic or global business arena, basically, business is a consumer-centric game of revenue and costs. Business architectures are built around their economic processes," said a senior business executive in the service industry. He concluded with the observation, "Given the complexities of global operations, to be effective a business model would have to be simple, sensible and sensitive to social, cultural and local consumer needs."

"Despite all the hype about business leadership, I feel a large number of future corporate models will be systems and performance led. Corporations will become more global and less national in their outlook. More performance focused and less personality focused. We have the know-how to incorporate performance indicators into the transnational multicultural corporation systems," said the CEO of a systems consultancy firm. After some elaborations he concluded with the observation: "Based on the inputs of global business-economic options, global positioning of individual corporate activities can also be optimised with appropriate global delivery systems. Management information systems may be designed to incorporate corporate health indicators as well as impact of key business drivers."

"Today, business wars are fought in many arenas with different weapons and thinking. Every business activity arena has its own rules, terrain, environment and competitors. Each requires a different strategic mindset. Depending on the situation, in the complex and dynamic competitive business environment, one requires unique and appropriate strategic alliances for organic or inorganic growth. Collaborative problem solving, co-operative research and resource sharing or collective implementations are various forms of strategic alliances. In all this, we need to be flexible and target focused," said a senior business consultant.

"Given the complexity of transnational cross-cultural global operations, I like to think in terms of a dynamically segregated layered structure for global corporations, especially for multiproduct and multiservice corporations. I like to think of simplicity as a strategy. Let me explain my concept. A team for each product or service operating in multiple national and local markets; they would develop their own global-local knowledge base and strategic think tank. In this way, each product would have its own global operational network. They would speak the same business language, understand global-local nuances. I would call this a business unit. Depending on the strategic advantages and comparative situations in different markets, the business units may operate in parallel, tandem, or in overlaid formations. The corporate office would coordinate and facilitate intra-corporate communication and knowledge sharing," said a senior manager in the auto industry.

"Given the imperatives of globalisation, today every company in the global and even domestic arena is busy trying to answer for itself, questions such as — how can we remain competitive? Build an effective team? Enhance our competitiveness? Hold on to our existing customers? How can we evolve a more effective corporate design? Build better products? Reduce costs? Optimise our business operations?

Enhance corporate intellectual capita? How to optimise organic-inorganic growth mix? These and many more such questions are on the agenda of most corporations around the world; all this with a global perspective," said a senior international business consultant.

After some discussions he went on to say, "Corporations have realised the imperatives of innovation and change management. Change is never easy, more so in the sensitive cross-cultural global context. Thus corporations are adopting innovation as a mindset — a thinking, a continuous process. It is no longer looked at as a stand-alone event." After some further discussions, he concluded with the following observation: "Among other things, a business leader today has to be a critical business analyser, an understanding facilitator for his team members and a strong advocate for his customers. Continuously innovating and changing as he moves along. However, at times, I feel, originality may be less important than usefulness — usefulness from the customers' perspective."

"Given the imperatives of globalisation and diversity, I feel global corporations should be revolutionary in their management thinking. Instead of trying to homogenise or regularise multinational diversity to create a homogeneous corporate culture, they should try to nurture diversity. They should let their corporate diversity diversify. In fact, I feel, they should encourage a creative clash of diversities in the especially created cyber corporate arena — an arena for corporate blurbing. Encourage clash of management and corporate thinking and debates on subjects such as, corporate growth options, strategy, global-local mix, new ideas and thoughts, corporate policy framework, identification and solution for internal corporate process inefficiencies or removal of corporate process constraints," said a senior lady business executive.

"Today, charting unfamiliar territory is the norm and not an exception. As corporations attempt to enhance their competitiveness, grow rapidly and create business values, each employee would be expected to find solutions to cross-cultural challenges and situations that have not been encountered earlier. In large globally matrixed organisations, the challenges get exponential in nature. The corporations are moved by the power of ideas and knowledge. The imperative of broad-basing corporate intellectual bases from departmental silos to global learning bases becomes obvious. Thus as I see it, the future corporate architectures and business models would be based on their knowledge imperatives. Corporations would create idea-receiving antenna-based structures and business processes. Corporations would aspire for effective networks that allow internal and external talented and entrepreneurial resources to constantly share and enhance their knowledge base and translate their learning into creating customer-focused business values," said a senior investment banker.

After some discussions he went on to say, "I like to think of future global business organisation models as dynamic, customer focused and competition-sensitive knowledge pools which are idea empowered and change oriented with perpetual and effective value adding systems."

"It may sound a bit un-businesslike, but from our Indian perspective, I feel we need to evolve a business model based on our historical and cultural values; enter the global arena with full business analysis but led by heartfelt emotions and intuitions. We need corporations empowered by global human values, emotions and intuitions for customer bonding; hardheaded business economics with genuine heartfelt local, social and cultural context, with a long-term emotional and commercial bonding, as one moves from one location to the next on the global canvas. I feel a global business model with local cultural contexts is possible and desirable. After all, all business is local. Customers are local. Customers define the rules and terms of business. Customers also define the competitive space. Organisational sensitivity to local needs, emotions and agility is critical for building successful relationships with customers," said the CEO of an emerging fashion house.

After explaining some of his concepts in detail he went on to say, "In the long run, individual, corporate and national identities are built on their real realities — their real actions and not on rhetoric. We need to get our business objectives, processes and implementations in harmony." After some elaborations he went on to say, "Now responding to your specific question, the business model that we hope to evolve may be explained as — local strategic bases with globally networked teams. Consumer imperatives are local. But we also need global inputs. This is how our global business model may evolve."

"We have to take into account the total dynamics of global environment. We need to understand the aggregate of all conditions affecting the existence, growth and welfare of international organisations. Also, I feel, we have to comprehend the dynamics of a corporate technology-enabled operational and distribution architecture. The game rules and competition are changing. Products are being wrapped in services and relationships. Corporations are shifting from product and service management to relationship management — relationship with customers, employees and business partners in a transnational and cross-cultural environment," said a senior partner of an international business consulting organisation.

After some discussions on the subject he went on to say, "Within the global business environment, context corporations have to work in locally segmented business environments. The corporate work cultural pyramid consists of global work culture, national work culture, corporate work culture and individual work culture."

"Business is a game of value addition — adding quality with other things remaining the same or cutting cost with other things remaining the same. With the available options of global sourcing, global processing and global marketing, corporations are in constant search for optimising their business processes or global business value chains. Given the fast-changing global business scenario, corporations are in a perpetual state of dynamic optimisation. Thus I would say that corporate designs and business models are in a permanent state of flux. What corporations need to take care of is their relationships with the societies in which they operate. I feel credible corporate governance is critical for a culturally sensitive global business arena. Societies would demand socio-economic accountability while the governments would need to protect the interests of their consumers," said a senior executive in the global logistics industry

"I visualise corporations as creative commercial energy centres; corporations knitting their own global networks. Commercial energy centres in search of sources to enhance their commercial energy. Corporations enhance their commercial energy by providing products and services to their customers at a profit. It comes from the process of relating with customers. Today by making use of the Internet and global connectivity, corporations can relate with customers in different parts of the world at their convenience. Thus corporations are constantly in search of ways to creatively relate with their customers to enhance customer satisfaction and in the process increase their own profits. The arena is global. The value chain is global. The opportunities are global. The customers are global. Thus the corporate structures are creativity led on the global stage," said the CEO of a dot.com organisation.

After elaborating on his points he went on to say, "Global corporations use blogs to interact with employees from different parts of the world and invite ideas from them. Blogs are also used to identify and rectify inefficiencies and constraints in the corporate business processes." After some further elaborations he said, "In the global context, the questions that a number of global corporations are asking are — should they replace expensive manpower by cheap manpower located in distant places or use software and global connectivity in restructuring their corporations? Also, with technology one is often faced with a choice between expensive and inefficient as well as centralisation and decentralisation; all this impacts the global business models."

"Whatever the corporate business model, the quality of corporate governance would be an area of concern where ever corporations operate. Corporations are the prime movers of economic change," said a senior business consultant. After some elaborations he went on to say, "Defined narrowly, corporate governance may be seen as a set of relationships between the company and shareholders; more often, a very limited number of shareholders. The broader definition covers the explicit relationships of the company with consumers, employees, distributors, creditors, government agencies and local communities; where ever they may operate. The beneficiary of good governance is every stakeholder. Good governance implies transparency in operations. With a steady increase in business literacy levels around the world, to be accepted locally, I feel, global corporations would have to evolve a credible framework of governance with local participation in formulating management policies as well as shareholders. Good corporate governance would have to be the handle to operate the competitive edge."

"Given the imperatives of globalisation and at times hypercompetition, a corporation for its own survival may have to be cold, impersonal and intolerant of individuality, creativity, imagination and autonomy; a soul destroying process. Yet at other times it may be searching for the highest standards of creative management. It is all situational. It would be unfair to judge a corporation with a snapshot perspective. The business operations and business priorities have to respond to the changing environment. Business models cannot be static," said a senior professor of a policy research institute.

"With the imperatives of globalisation, I feel all industries are changing and their borders are blurring. Even the definitions of industries are changing. It is becoming more and more difficult to demarcate, quantify or identify the nature of competition faced by individual industries. Business models and management job profiles are in a state of flux. To speak in general terms would be very misleading. To make a meaningful statement, I will have to be industry and situation specific," said a senior business partner of a global consultancy organisation.

"Corporations, as I visualise, in the global business arena are evolving into modular networked frameworks, both internally as well as externally. Within corporations, each business process is being analysed from its knowledge-skill-technology perspective. It is compacted as a job-process capsule. Then the company looks for the most economic location on the global scene to locate it. The set-of-jobs or the business process is shipped out to the most economic location. The scale, speed and structures of corporations are changing fast. Corporations have become more economic sensitive due to competition. One has to understand the business economics of each link in the corporate global value chain. In a transactional industry like ours, broadly the jobs are divided into customer-interface jobs, customer service support jobs and back office jobs. Thus I feel the new business models are spread all over the world. Technology is redefining jobs. As is popularly said, corporations are increasingly operating in a flat world with flat structures," said a senior executive in the investment banking industry.

"I believe an organisation design depends on the nature of business and economic circumstances in which a company operates. Also, I feel, organisation design and organisation behaviour are interdependent. Vitality of a business model can be gauged from the way in which executives of the organisation adopt, adapt, adjust and respond to internal changes and external challenges. We need to understand the critical measures for efforts, efficiency and effectiveness adopted by organisations. Overall, I think, it is a feeling reflected through growth and industry-specific leadership, demonstrated by individual corporations," said a senior business consultant.

"While all kinds of business models in different industries are evolving, with new job profiles, I think for some time, notwithstanding the financial crisis, the two most popular industries for B-school graduates will continue to be management consultancy and investment banking — I-bank as it is popularly called. Both industries offer social status, global options, growth and matching rewards. However, within these two industries there are wide spectrums of job-profiles. In consultancy, assignments may similarly range from proactively helping clients enhance their growth prospects to providing research and data support to front-end client interface teams. Similarly, in I-bank scope of assignments, jobs may range from providing implementation consultancy to clients in areas such as corporate finance; mergers and acquisitions; trading in equity, securitization of bonds or derivatives to selling financial products and back-office activities. The job profiles keep changing," said a placement officer of a leading B-school.

After elaborating on his experience with various B-schools he went on to say, "The qualities and personal traits most well-known companies are looking for in their recruits include, a positive attitude; the ability to build relationships; empathy based on appreciation of the client's concerns and capacity for hard work as well as competency to work under pressure. I feel corporations do not give much importance to academic results. Also, as we know, placement is a critical factor for student preference of B-schools; keeping the end in mind, we give relatively less importance to academic scores and more to future placement potential characteristics of candidates at the time of selecting our students."

After some further elaboration he continued, "From my perspective, I see corporations in the global transactional industries evolving into three dimensional matrix structures with focus being on, country or region if the countries are relatively small; business sector; and specific activity. Within each of these, there is an implicit and explicit dynamics of global-local in brands, products and services; centralisation-decentralisation in designing global organisational structures; and human talent-technology mix depending on local business landscape, while maintaining customer focus. In order to facilitate each business activity to grow in its own optimal ways, the head office tries to evolve a scaleable convergent infrastructure for the organisation as a whole."

After explaining some of his observations he summed up with the following statement: "The global business arena is a learning arena, and learning corporations are always in search of ethereal knowledge and information. There is so much diversity, so much to learn. Today business is a dynamic game of learning, unlearning and relearning."

"After having worked in my home country for the same company for many years, I have entered the global business arena with apprehension. This is my second international assignment. With my limited experience, I feel we have a lot to learn about the local markets. Instead of imposing our national brands on other local markets, we first need to understand the local business culture, markets and customers. Since we only know our products, our brands and our ways of selling, we usually try imposing or creatively hard selling our products in local markets, often disregarding many local values and customer expectations. I think this is being done by many multinationals, even by those who have been here for many years. Perhaps it is part of the globalisation process or corporate desire to make this world unicultured or flat. Well one does talk about *glocal* (global-local) localisation of global products and services but I feel we need to go *locglo* (local-global). Start with the local first. Start with the local base to match global products to local business culture and values. Localise the global products. Also, add global values to local products and services. I do not know if I have been able to explain, but I do see some major differences in the two processes. We need to respect local market values and customer ethos. We need to gain insights of the local markets and customers. Given the cultural diversity and variety of local business models, it is a daunting task. Frankly I am awed by it all. I am not in position to make a firm statement on the questions you have asked," said an expat vice-president of a large transnational corporation.

After elaborating on some points he said, "I feel we cannot take the present flow of globalisation for granted. With my limited interactions in different parts of the world, I feel capitalism, market economy or even growth does not mean the same thing to different people and communities in different parts of the world."

After explaining some of his concepts, he went on to say, "Every high growth economic process has a life span. Using their money power, corporations are able to get their way with national leaders and the people in power in different countries but the national grassroots are often on different wavelengths. Globalisation does not generate happiness, goodwill or prosperity for every one. This is true even for the rich developed countries. For global growth, based on global goodwill and understanding, I feel corporations more so large global corporations need to think of themselves as multicultural social organisations and not just unicultural business corporations."

After further elaborating on some of the above topics, he went on to say, "About the future global scenario and global corporate structures, I feel each large global company will emerge as a global framework with deep local roots. All globalisation is local. Local cultures are too critical to be ignored for too long. Unless the corporate global-local mix becomes an integral part of the local culture, as has happened in Europe for some products, corporations may not feel very comfortable. Corporations have to become an integral part of local social happenings."

Speaking on a similar theme, the vice-president of another transnational organisation said, "I feel corporations will become less national and more global in their composition, human resources and policy frameworks. Today, as in the case of individuals, we think of corporations as German, Japanese or American corporations; we identify them by their nation of origin. For business executives, it is an age of divided loyalties. Think of an Indian executive working for a German company in Japan. Global shared values would be the only way to hold stakeholders together. As globalisation gains ground, national ethos would have to give way to global shared values and beliefs with benevolent and humane management; personal integrity, fairness, decency and respect for individuals; warmth, ethical conduct and meticulous concern for quality. Corporations would either adopt these policies or face cultural backlash. Currently most large MNCs tend to just focus on business issues and are protocol oriented."

After some further elaborations he went on to say, "I cannot answer some of your questions; I don't know the answers. Some of them are new for me and I need time to study, think and develop my response. With all my readings and experience, I feel, there are many gaps in our knowledge about the understanding of the world of business. B-schools need to do some credible and serious research on the ownership patterns, organisational structures, control mechanisms, stakeholders' concerns and governance of global corporations. B-schools need to transform themselves from just skill imparting institutes to also evolving as knowledge hubs of fast-changing global business operations."

"Corporations are a sum total of their various job-activity capsules. Given the technology options and various global business delivery models, most job modules can be transported to any part of the world. Keeping in view the shifting economic advantages, perhaps modular corporate structures would be most appropriate and competitive. New business will develop around the technologies that are with us and those under development. We are yet to make full use of the options available in use of IT, ITeS and communication technologies in areas such as education, healthcare or global corporate designs," said the senior vice-president of an international IT corporation.

"Notwithstanding, all the talk about globalisation, global sourcing, outsourcing and multisourcing, I feel the future corporation will be more closely integrated and customer focused. For appropriate consumer focus, we have to creatively slice and dice the global markets on the basis of factors such as psychographics, demographics and cultural profiles. Today we have the technologies and global connectivity to integrate and synchronise diverse global corporate operations to navigate in the global business arena with the corporate compass firmly focused on customers. Given the global digital options I don't see why corporations need the traditional middlemen like advertising agencies for their marketing operations. Marketing needs to be a seamless integrated part of corporate operations. Frankly, based on my experience in marketing operations in different countries, I have often found advertising agencies as the weakest link in marketing operations. Marketing operations need to be customer focused and more responsive to customer needs with a long-term perspective. Corporations need to continuously upgrade marketing intellectual capital by assimilating consumer insights. Corporate and marketing communications should be an integral part of corporate operations. I feel it is too critical a role to be outsourced," said a senior vice-president in the automobile industry.

After elaborating on some of the points he went on to say, "I feel, there is an obvious economic and business disconnect between corporate business objectives and those of advertising agencies, even in their short-term and long-term perspectives."

After further elaborating on some of his experiences in the auto industry he went on to say, "We have a lot of data about consumers, both current and potential. We are constantly learning but also have a fairly good idea about consumer behaviour and expectations. Using data about consumers, internet options and computer algorithms we can reach our messages to individual consumers on their computers, cell phones and televisions. We can even make it personal and interactive. We need to move away from mass advertising to individualised and personalised communications. The need for constant learning, updating and adapting new strategies to interact with customers requires internalisation of customer relations and communication. Thus I feel corporations will see the advantage in integrating their global operations yet serving customers with local emotions and smiles."

After further elaborations he went on to say, "With my limited experience, I can only speak for the auto industry, but I have a feeling that what is true for us in this industry may also be applicable in other industries such as hospitality, air travel, healthcare and banking." He concluded with the following observation: "Like the media purchase companies to expand their marketing operations, some corporations may opt for retail space purchase for their products and services to gain visibility advantage."

Reflecting similar thoughts, a professor of corporate communication said, "Given the diversity and sensitivities of the global business area, I feel transnational corporations need to develop well thought out global integrated corporate communication plans, projecting long-term perspectives with cross-cultural internal harmony. My limited research indicates that outsourcing and limited internal involvements often contribute to internal cynicism. Also, economic dynamics and critical role of corporate communications in various forms and different customer interface situations warrant an integrated global communication perspective."

Speaking on similar lines, a senior business consultant said, "Globalisation process and corporate global architecture of any organisation rests on its local pillars. To maintain customer focus, imperatives of localisation cannot be overlooked." He went on to further elaborate, "Multinational corporations will transform from national corporate culture to the global mindset slowly. The global economics will force them to locate their different corporate activities to wherever they are done best. Transnational corporations, I feel, will evolve as dynamic mini-global communities, with a synergistic local-global mix. For sustainable competitiveness, the global corporations, I think, would evolve into a collage of distinct local hues and colours." After some elaboration he went on to say, "I feel local cultures have to be given due consideration in global operations. Also with globalisation, local cultures would try hard to retain their identity. Trying to globalise local cultural ethos may prove counterproductive for multinational corporations."

"We have to move towards higher productivity. Our corporations have to attain global productivity standards. They must try to gain competitive advantages by aiming for world efficiency standards and not continue to rely on advantages based on low wages due to our poverty standards. Productivity gains help workers, corporations and nations," said a professor of economics. After explaining his concepts in some detail he went on to say, "Notwithstanding our achievements in information technology and space, pharmaceuticals and biotechnology, we must remember that ours is basically an agrarian economy. Indian corporations as they grow and expand will have an urban-rural mix. I strongly feel our corporate focus must include agriculture and agro-based industries in their various extended operations."

"In the future corporate philosophy, I feel education or talent development would be an integral part of corporate thinking and corporate operations. I feel there is a need for new dynamic, need and technology-based models in education. While the world and we have moved from an agricultural economy, to industrial economy, to service economy and now to information and knowledge era, our education system still remains steeped in the old format. We are not making use of our new technologies in education. With an ocean full of information on the Internet, today one can educate oneself, yet the education system continues to rely on old techniques and methods. I am not an educationalist, but feel there must be huge scope for the education system to improve its reach and productivity by adopting ITeS and communication technologies in education. I do not know what is holding us back in experimenting with it on the local, state or national level," said a senior lady executive of an NGO operating in rural areas.

After explaining some of her concerns she went on to say, "Given the enormity of the problem of imparting education, it is time to explore all possible avenues. Lack of proper education is a real curse on our society. There is so much wastage and lack of concern in the general public. We need to use our technical know-how resources in effective ways to improve our living conditions. We need to evolve new education models. Industries, keeping in view their future needs, need to create their own talent resources."

"Schools, colleges and universities around the world need to realign their education products to meet the needs of changing times. They also need to take a global perspective of education. The developed regions of the world are losing some jobs to the developing countries. Developed countries also have to restructure their education system to prepare new talent streams to meet their own future talent requirements in their countries. Universities as academic service providers, like other service providers, need to take a global view of their own value chains and go global, as well as adapt their academic service offerings to the local-global needs," said a senior international education consultant.

"As we prepare for our future, I feel we must also ask: what have we done with our history, land, historical inheritance, rivers and mountains; our cultural heritage, archaeological treasures and our civilisation? I feel we often have to consult our past to visualise our future," said a university professor.

"I have often wondered, what would a future corporation of my dreams be? A multicultural, multi-ethnic, multireligious corporation full of knowledge, compassion, competitiveness and spirituality; in perpetual internal as well as external harmony. A happiness-generating corporation in sync with human happiness around the world. Is it possible?" After elaborating on some of her observations, a lady CEO of an NGO went on to say, "Do we have corporate *kundalini*? Does the concept of self-actualisation and self-realisation apply to corporations? Is there a corporate yoga? What is the Zen of corporate zest?" After some discussions she went on to say, "I feel as corporations are a sum total of their human capital, there is a need to examine issues like corporate diet and yoga; corporate calorie intake and consumption. Corporations also become overweight or too thin. Corporations also need to take care of their shapes, knowledge bases and intellectual levels."

As we interacted with various experts and executives engaged in the global business operations, few corporate concerns became apparent. A number of global corporations are in search of paradigms and solutions to optimise their global operations. Potentials of available technology options are yet to be realised and exploited in many industries. The challenges and opportunities remain unrealised in many cases due to the lack of availability of appropriate talent. Keeping this in mind, we moved on to the perceptions of talent needs.

7

The Global Talent Hunt

"For talent hunt, we go around the world, visit the best known business schools looking for potential proactive business leaders. It is the people who guide, identify new growth areas, develop and make corporations competitive in the global business arena. I like to stress on the proactive characteristics, because I feel basically it is the proactive nature that separates managers from business leaders," said a senior human resource manager of a large multinational corporation.

After explaining his perceptions and reasons for his preference for proactive executives, he went on to say, "I tend to evaluate the proactive learning nature of potential candidates by their learning attitude towards their own selected hobbies as well as from their ability to ask perceptive questions. For me a perceptive question from a potential candidate carries more weight than a right response."

After further elaborating on the above points, he went on to say, "I think it is a natural attribute and is very difficult to develop at a later phase in the career. The proactive trait is often misunderstood during our childhood and in the prevailing education system. Even B-schools with their emphasis on rote teaching and learning, tend to harm this critical attribute of potential managers. One thing that is a definite no-no for me is a pre-determined textbook answer to a topical observation or question during interviews."

"I feel we need greater focus on vocational training. We need flexible schooling where children can have vocational education at an early stage and determine their areas of vocational interests. Yet they should be able to change streams if they develop interest in new areas. After all, life is a venture in new mental and emotional explorations. Let me clarify my definition; by vocational training for children I mean giving them some awareness and a general feel of job activities in business operations. The emphasis should be on interest-based employability or self-employment," said a human resource manager.

After further elaborations he went on to say, "You may be shocked and surprised, but I look for an intuitive enthusiastic smile on the faces of graduates of B-schools. Unfortunately it is not easy to find. Our overall stress-generating education system along with B-schools with their structured pedagogy and pre-determined teaching programmes, tend to demolish the instincts and enthusiasm of students. During my interview interactions, I try to explore if any sparks are still there. At times I feel our education system tends to destroy the natural learning instincts and enthusiasm of students." He concluded with the following observation: "We need and value people with a purpose. A corporate system only specifies work. People give it life and purpose."

"Our search for talent starts and ends with the search for managers who have a proactive purpose in life. A target. An objective. They add value to the corporate energy pool. Managers without objectives I feel are corporate drags. They consume vital corporate energies. For us, good managers are those who put in their professional best to achieve organisational goals while optimising on their own objectives as well as of their colleagues and employees whose work they supervise. They are able to creatively align their own goals and those of their team members with the corporate goals," said a senior human resource manager of a global business consultancy organisation.

Speaking on similar lines, another human resource manager of a large multinational organisation said, "Talent means different things to different corporations. Talent is job and situation specific. Each organisation is in search of talent that it needs. Even when different organisations visit the same B-school or any other human resource base, they are searching for a different talent mix. Here we need to see each organisation as a unique and dynamic talent-mix entity. Besides various other factors, its talent-mix depends on the nature of its industry, its own business traditions and future strategic outlook. Each organisation is unique in every way as we are, as individuals. In general terms, when an organisation goes on a talent hunt, its aim is to advance or enhance its average level of talent. It has a fair idea of its weak areas, current needs and future-anticipated requirements."

After explaining some of his concepts, he went on to say, "My outlook depends on the teams for which I have to select new members. Keeping in mind the tempo of work, team structures and the prevailing interpersonal relationships, I search for the best-fit who will improve productivity, team cohesiveness as well as the overall performance of the team. While searching for a specific skill or talent, we have to often compromise as skill-possessing candidates come as total individuals with all their personal characteristics."

"Academic performance of candidates in B-school subjects is of little importance to me. We have very extensive in-house training programmes. Notwithstanding all our efforts to be objective, our selections are prejudiced by the reputation of the B-school; like other corporations we also have internal corporate caste system, group preferences and alumni groupings. It creates all sorts of loyalty-performance evaluation conflicts," said a senior human resource manager of a global consumer goods organisation.

After some discussions he added, "Now to answer your question as to why we go for a reputed brand of B-school and not for the best talent. There is some logic and a few historical compulsions. First, as I said we do have an internal 'caste' system. It helps if the new entrant fits in with the established caste structure. Also most reputed B-schools have a structured selection procedure. It facilitates our screening. Although their screening criteria are different from the ones we may use for different jobs but it is somewhat helpful. Notwithstanding all the drawbacks, do we have a better option? To respond to your charge that we may be being less than professional in opting for a brand, as an easy option, rather than knowledgeable professionals who could identify performers from any source, there is some truth in it. Frankly we are being less than professional in our selection process based on B-school brands."

After some discussions, he went on to say, "There is no doubt that the failure of critical thinking continues to be perpetuated by an educational system that insists on learning by rote." After some further elaborations he summed up with the following observation: "All said and done, B-school brands do help us enhance our corporate brands with clients also. Like every other established brand there is an air and aura of reliability."

"I have no hesitation in saying that the prevailing B-school scenario is far from desirable. We all — corporations, B-schools, clients and consumers seem to be trapped in the vicious cycle of historical global brand preferences, a global-brand syndrome. Notwithstanding the many failures, the blind fundamentalist belief that Harvard Mckinsey combine can do no wrong prevails. It all seems to have become an integral part of our corporate thinking. Yes, the corporations are paying the price in terms of low performance. Internal alumni networking or groups of various B-schools have often proved harmful. B-school networking often subjugates real performance. A lot of halo affect prevails. Because of this, much corporate inefficiency exists in various corporations. As we all know it has even resulted in some major corporate failures. But, again I don't know a way out of it," said the CEO of a leading headhunting organisation.

After some discussions on the above points, he went on to say, "I feel it is time for us to be honest about the real realities of B-schools. As an alumnus of a globally well-known business school, let me ask you — how do students prioritise B-schools? What do B-schools sell? I may be wrong but from my own experience and that of my friends, I can say that B-schools sell themselves and are selected on the basis of short-term cost-benefit analysis or a return on total investment (ROTI) perception. B-schools talk of placements, not learning. Going to a B-school is a business contract. It seems to be a fee-for-job understanding."

After some more elaborations he went on to say, "As management and entrepreneurship teaching institutes, B-schools, even some of the best ones, may be rated poorly in self-management, governance, transparency, social responsibility, resource utilisation, change management, research, creativity and innovation. From my experience, I feel B-schools are system oriented rather than substance. Thinking of students as their customers, they are more focused on student satisfaction rather than real learning. We need to take a holistic view of B-school operations and their human resource development processes. I look at recruitment from B-schools as a raw talent mining process, not as a finished product."

"The recent global business debacle should be an eye-opener for us. Even the global monitoring and corporate rating organisations with hundreds of bright B-school graduates form the best B-schools in the world failed to foresee the debacle. They were the lead players. No early warnings came from them, nor did the warnings come from the best of B-schools. Why couldn't they see it coming? In fact dangerous, about-to-erupt business volcanoes were rated as desirable risk-free zones by them," said a retired army general who had also been the director of a B-school. After some elaborations he went on to say, "The attitude towards the culture of intellectual curiosity that the academia adopts gets reflected in the work culture it produces. The prevailing B-school system stifles intellectual curiosity. We need an honest and a systematic analysis of the management education system."

"There is a lot of talk about talent gap but little talk of specifics. Which corporations need what kind of talent, why, and what are they doing about it? As I see it, talent is job specific and has a limited life span. Talent has to be defined and directed — be it knowledge base, skill set or attitude oriented. For long-term sustainability it needs to be continuously nurtured. At times it seems to me that corporations or their CEOs seem to just sit back and grumble. Even their business associations talk about it in seminars but do little to resolve the issue. I do not know of any business association that has come up with an action-oriented solution blueprint with a time frame. Industry, educational organisations and the government need to work out a comprehensive plan. Evolve a curriculum and pedagogy. Make use of prevailing technologies to transform human resource into human capital and create an appropriate national talent pool. We have to shift from rhetoric to road map," said a senior professor of an engineering college.

Speaking on similar lines, another professor of a leading business school said, "What we need to introduce in our education is a three-year degree in business technology. The curriculum of this degree should include comprehensive education in management subjects as well as use of information technology. About six months of interactions with business organisations should be an integral part of the degree requirements. The graduating students would then be industry ready. Corporations can and should provide their need-specific orientation to their selected candidates.

Their careers can be nurtured by e-learning, in-house training, need-based occasional seminars and workshops."

After explaining some of his suggestions, he went on to say, "I feel corporations need to create their own talent development centres with outside experts as occasional visitors. After a few years of experience in the corporate world, if needed, corporations may sponsor their candidates to some business school of their choice for a short-term degree course; relating experience to academics and synergising learning for growth. The same approach may be adopted for executives in the technical areas of corporate activities." He concluded with the following observation: "Perhaps management education and engineering subjects should be introduced at the high school level."

Speaking on similar lines, a senior business consultant said, "Instead of talent hunts, corporations need to evolve their own need-specific talent development approach. Instead of corporate formulated training programmes and career paths, they should let employees opt for proactive self-education and training. Keeping in view the corporate growth areas and directions, corporations should let employees create their learning road maps, knowledge approach routes and learning speed zones to enhance their competencies and competitiveness. In a competitive world all have to compete proactively."

Speaking on similar lines, a senior executive in the software industry said, "I feel business units need a corporate wide *kaizen* policy — a clearly stated and communicated corporate policy. The *Kaizen* approach to cut costs, improve quality and enhance customer satisfaction. With appropriate corporate systems, by proactive individual efforts of employees, this will automatically result in improving the corporate intellectual base. This will also enhance corporate capabilities and competencies. I feel this is what talent need and talent development is all about."

"The war for talent is on. It will continue to be there. Good managers will always be in short supply. Corporations will continue to seek more from their limited resources. We need to ask ourselves — what kind of talent will the corporations need? What would be the nature and profile of dreamers and can-do implementers which the corporation would be searching for? We need to think of talent with a dynamic future perspective for each industry. We need to do serious thinking on this issue. Talent mismatch may result in very serious and expensive mistakes," said a senior executive in a research and development organisation.

"The reason why companies keep on talking about talent shortages but do little to correct the situation is limitations of their own serious thinking. Based on my experience, I feel there has been very little creative and innovative thinking in appropriate sourcing and developing talent. Corporations suffer from internal communication gaps. Market forces and technology have impacted many job specifications. Corporate internal processes keep changing. But the contents and formats of management information systems (MIS) and decision support systems (DSS) remain the same. We overlook the fact that MIS and DSS have a limited life span. They are target and situation specific," said a senior business consultant.

After explaining some of his concepts, he went on to say, "Just take a closer look at the recruitment and training policies of the corporations. With all the talk of changes in business environment, technology transformations and business paradigm shifts, how different are the recruitment procedures and training policies of the corporations? The sourcing, selection criteria and placement policies continue to be almost same. Why have majority of corporations ignored the use of information technology in in-house training? With all the talk of the critical role of knowledge in strategic and competitive advantages, why do corporations not incorporate management education as a continuous learning process in their scheme of management? How many corporations have appropriate and objective performance evaluation systems?"

"I feel there are many reasons for high rates of churning. Some of the reasons are of our own creation. To attract potential employees we make use of advertising. As in the case of products and other services, the advertising messages for jobs also tend to sell virtual dreams. When the candidates join the company after selection, they are disillusioned and disappointed by the real nature of the job," said a lady human resource manager of a large multinational organisation.

After discussing some of her recent case examples, she went on to say, "Business schools reinforce the problem, by giving an exaggerated view of the business world. I remember when we used to do case studies in class; we used to feel like real decision makers or corporate leaders, heroes and warriors. We came out so elated, congratulating ourselves on our own logic or statements. Since there were no real results we were all winners." After a short pause she said with a smile, "But now we all know that the real business world is so very different."

"I feel management education teaching by B-schools, their training objectives, the skills and perceptions imparted by them are mostly sales focused, more or less for field or market areas. The transformational side of business gets little attention in B-schools. They are mainly transactional-activity (sales) oriented. Frankly, I feel, manufacturing is very low on their agenda. Thus I feel my views on management education or B-schools or talent development would have limited value, if any. Out talent needs are technical in nature and job specific," said a senior manager of a large manufacturing unit

Speaking on the topic of churning and performance, the senior vice-president of a multinational investment bank said, "There are all kinds of jobs in different organisations. However, as I understand, the two areas of preference in most B-schools are consultancy and investment banking. Even when students join in these areas, they face some severe emotional turmoil. The fancy images created by the high profile historic case studies come in conflict with the real ground realities. First the real jobs are less glamorous and more demanding in the real terms. For those interacting with clients, they have to cope with demands of individual clients as well as corporate objectives. Then they have their teams, targets and internal competition with their colleagues. The other jobs tend to be demanding in their own ways and may tend to be repetitive also. With my experience I can say, B-schools do not prepare their students for the real realities of the jobs they aspire."

After some discussion on the various job profiles he said, "Based on the knowledge bases, skill sets and attitudes or mindsets required for different jobs, I would broadly demarcate corporate personnel into four broad categories — soldiers or workers, managers, business leaders and entrepreneurs. There are a large number of jobs that have to be done with the spirit and attitude of soldiers, the do-as-told jobs. Then there are jobs for those who manage or get work done from soldiers. Depending on company policy, entry levels may vary. Here they may be required to do some related assignments also. The third category is that of business leaders; those who lead their teams, departments or divisions to higher performance levels. They are positioned on the bases of their proven experience and performance. They operate within the historical or defined-activity boundaries. The fourth group is that of entrepreneurs; they take the corporations to new areas of business activities or develop new ways of doing business to relate to new customers or to old customers more effectively. All these require different sets of knowledge bases, skill sets and mindsets. The number of jobs in each category are also defined by the nature of business. B-schools tend to go by the one-size-fits-all philosophy in their programmes. I hope this answers your question on why we often tend to position and pay different salaries to students from the same batch while they may have gone through the same selection and education process. Perhaps you may like to look at it from a different perspective — we are looking for intrinsic qualities of an individual and not the skills acquired in B-schools. This is also supported by the fact that there is no correlation between academic performance at B-school and job profile or the compensations offered to graduates from the same class."

After some more discussions on the topic he said, "Frankly I do not like the word 'administration' in the degree Master of Business Administration (MBA). In today's dynamic world, one has to think in terms of proactive management and optimisation of resource usage in the overall development context. We need to question our assumptions and examine our terms of references, anew. Our environmental parameters and options are changing fast."

"For us the basic difference between the working philosophy of B-schools and us is that while they are focused on imparting hard or technical skills, be it in marketing, finance, human resource management, international business operations, information technology or any other area of their specialisation, we are more focused on soft skills," said the senior lady vice-president of a multinational bank. After elaborating on the above point, she went on to say, "Hard skills are corporate specific. Hard-skill mix needs, to a large extent, depend on unique corporate business processes and their strategic orientation. During our corporate training sessions, B-school graduates have to go through an extensive unlearning process. Teaching soft skills becomes very difficult. Many B-school graduates lack even the basic interpersonal communication skills. I may sound fastidious to you, but they often lack general business etiquette, business dress sense or how to greet with a smile or the use of common courtesies. These are very critical in cross-cultural interactions. We even have to teach them the use of words such as thank you and sorry. Some of these soft skills are quite difficult to teach to grown-ups and mature business graduates. I personally feel imparting a sense of business discipline and sensitivities towards cross-cultural etiquettes should form an integral part of the B-school curriculum."

"What I miss most and value highly when hunting for talent is, innate enthusiasm for the overall business game. Not only most B-school graduates tend to have a very narrowly focused perception of business, mostly of their selected specialisation, they also often lack interest and knowledge in other related business activity areas. They usually talk of business activities such as finance, marketing, human resource management and information technology as if they were separate, segregated and unrelated activities. We have to look at business operations as a whole — as an overall integrated process."

She concluded with the following observation: "What we look for and need are executives with an overall view of business processes and appreciation for their own role in it; people with passion for professional excellence and for them to be effective team players with consumer empathy; or people with enthusiasm for a game called business."

As we discussed the talent issue with various headhunters and executives from different organisations, we tried to conceptualise and design an alternate approach or paradigm to management education. Our primary objective or purpose was to reduce the identified gaps between the capabilities and competencies of B-school graduates and the corporate needs; thus the effort to optimise on talent development process in the management education areas.

8

Nurturing Proactive Business Performers

Our multiple interactions with various B-school graduates as well as faculty members — some with high individual global brand equity, did not provide any significant differentiations between the prevalent school and university pedagogy and that adopted by business schools. Many emphatically stated that the use of historical case studies was in no way unique to business schools. The difference, if any, many surmised was market created, the result of product differentiation efforts. Overall, B-schools were more similar than different.

Whatever the reasons — economic, market or historical — for management education to be perceived, treated and valued so differently from other education streams, we were keen to search for ways to add value and make management education more relevant for industry and its users. Having heard of the gaps between B-school outputs and industry requirements, we were keen to find ways to add some intrinsic value to management education. This chapter is an effort in that direction.

As stated in earlier chapters, during our interactions with the various business executives, some cynically surmised that B-schools making use of their expertise in brand building and product differentiations have been able to craft and perpetuate differentiations to their advantage. Directly or indirectly their queries included — what do the B-schools really sell? What do corporations procure from B-schools? What are the institutional social responsibilities demonstrated by B-schools? What could be the appropriate qualifications for B-school faculty? Why is there a perpetual acute shortage of appropriately qualified faculty for B-schools? What have the B-schools done about it? What are the advantages and disadvantages associated with evaluation of B-school faculty and its pedagogy? What are the approaches and mindsets of B-schools on local-global issues? What is the utility and evaluation of faculty development programmes of B-schools? What are the unique local-global requirements and the standardisation trends in B-schools? What are the appropriate critical performance indicators for B-schools? What knowledge bases, skill sets and mindsets are business school graduates expected to have? Is there governance and transparency in business school operations? What are the objectives of information and communication policies adopted by B-schools? What are the norms for business school governance? How to evaluate the quality and relevance of research, creativity, innovation, development and consultancy activities of business schools? These and may such questions had cropped up during our interactions with different people associated with management education.

Some often expressed their concerns: "Just as good education helps societies, irrelevant education may also harm societies. How do we differentiate between useful and harmful management education? How do the benefits co-relate with the costs of education in B-schools?"

Although most of the people we contacted were not happy with the academic processes and output of B-schools, they also expressed their inability to suggest an alternative approach. With humility, we are making an effort to present an alternative — an alternative to think anew.

We feel an educational institution is basically about learning. Learning to learn and think. A good educational institute should provide effective impetus to proactive learning, mentor proactive learning processes, and provide effective learning support systems. Shore up learning processes that motivate further learning — learning that helps us discover our own potential; our own sense of being.

Business Schools: Evaluation criterion

Parameters commonly used to evaluate and rank B-schools include — infrastructure, intellectual capital, admissions criterion, placements, industry interface and governance.

Except for placements, perhaps performance evaluation parameters used for other professional institutes would be similar. Placements by B-schools are usually referred to in terms of salaries offered to their graduates by the industry at the end of their academic programme and not in terms of the real earnings value-added by the B-school programme. Input-output or cost benefit ratios are not talked about.

Also one seldom hears about the quality of assignments or the variance in salaries offered to different students in the same batch. With a large number of students seeking admissions and with the application of high quality control procedures adopted for input selection, teaching and evaluation, how does one explain the vast variances in output — the large differences in salaries offered to graduates of the same batch by corporations in the same industry? What is the correlation between performance of students in B-schools and in the business arena?

During our various interviews, some of the other questions that keep cropping up included — why are business schools given so much importance by the media and society? Is it because of the critical nature of management or due to the role played by business organisations in our society? Is it a self-serving myth perpetuated by the alumni? Do we really know what is the real value being added by different business schools?

The above questions seem reasonable as input-output ratio analysis, study of core competencies and quality control systems form an integral part of B-schools' curricula. After all, performance evaluation is an integral part of management learning programmes.

The Value Chain

The students to business schools come from various different disciplines. Like most other professional institutes, pedagogy used by B-schools includes — case studies, faculty lectures, some surprise tests, project assignments to students, guest speakers from the industry and some direct and indirect interface with industry.

Also, as in business, B-schools follow-the-leader and adopt curriculum as well as pedagogy of their market leader. Currently, most B-schools use the same or similar pedagogy — case studies, analytical tools, presentation techniques, books, project assignments and student evaluation processes. This makes the B-school programmes almost a standard *service-product*; one-size-fits-all approach. Ironically, majority of the faculty members teaching future managers have little or no industry or managerial experience themselves. Thus, more often swimming is taught by experts who have never been in water.

Rote teaching-learning is common in B-schools. The durations of the coveted MBA degree usually varies between one and two academic years or about 500 hours to about 1,200 classroom hours.

An Industry Perspective

Business units operate in a dynamic, fast-changing environment. One often hears of change, more change and more multifaceted change. Corporate speak includes out-of-the-box thinking; hypercompetition; creativity; the nitty-gritty of competitive business processes; need for new and more competitive business models; innovative value adding global value chains; reducing lifecycles of products; falling brand advantages; proactive change and innovation management; shifting job-profiles; global perspectives and local understanding; cross-cultural sensitivities; dynamics of domain knowledge, skill sets and mindset shifts. They often express their search for proactive strategic mindsets, self-motivated go getters, opportunity spotting talents, innovative and creative value adding solution finders.

When asked, corporates often cite the lack of effective team players as a major constraint to their growth. The supply constraint is not so much of quantity but more of quality. Recruits from B-schools have to be put through unlearning and re-learning processes before they are termed as job-fit.

Notwithstanding the fact that corporations spend valuable resources in selecting, inducting and re-training their new management resources, even a cursory glance at the career paths of the majority of B-school alumni highlights random waywardness.

Disconnect between B-school output and Business needs

It is not uncommon to find articles by eminent business players reiterating and elaborating on the lines of the famous books — *What they don't teach you at Harvard Business School* and *What they really teach you at the Harvard Business School*. Notwithstanding the ongoing debate on the subject, most of the people we interacted with expressed that there is a need to re-construct curriculum of B-schools and align pedagogy with the fast-changing real realities of dynamic fast-changing information and knowledge era business operations, so as to make the MBA students industry and job fit.

With the prevailing imperatives of globalisation, global sourcing and outsourcing, continual impact of disruptive technologies and business models, global connectivity, empowerment of customers and Internet-based knowledge support systems, it may not be inappropriate to critically examine the potential role and contribution of business schools in the evolving business milieu.

Also, as expressed by various management education observers, given the dynamics of globalisation and simultaneous need for localisation in the hypercompetitive, fast changing and sensitive cross-cultural business environment, the need for future-sensitive business executives with appropriate knowledge bases, skill sets, mindsets and attitudes cannot be overstated. In the fast-changing knowledge era, rote teaching and learning based on industrial-age experiences is likely to be unproductive, if not harmful. To be effective, learning in a fast-changing business environment has to be proactive and enthusiastic situation-based learning, not one-size-fits-all imposed teaching.

It is a common observation that rote teaching creates risk-averse students. We need new ways to look at change and learning. Experiment with various forms of experimental learning methods.

Whatever we may call it — the sub-prime crisis, credit crisis, financial crisis or the global economic crisis — it substantiates the fact that we need a new management philosophy. The current MBA paradigm has aged. The status-quo needs change.

To align B-schools with the real realities of the business arena, perhaps it is time for a paradigm shift or need for re-engineering B-school teaching-learning processes. Perhaps we need to redefine and contextualise management education. With all humility, we propose the following framework.

Morphing B-schools into B-learning Centres

Perhaps, to effectively connect business and B-schools we need to shift our focus from teaching to proactive learning of business students — changing B-school DNA from teaching to learning mode. The shift would include:

Future Business Managers

Given the availability of internet, 24x7 global connectivity and information-empowered customers, it may not be inappropriate to think of graduate business school students (B-school customers) as informed observers of management operations. Before joining B-schools, they would have experienced being direct targets of various business promotion activities. Faced innumerable advertisements directed at them. They would have experienced at home, with friends and in the marketplaces various facets of integrated marketing communications, accounting, finance, planning, organising, leadership, control, customer and interpersonal relationship management. They would be information and communication technology savvy. They would have also experienced budget control systems, time management, quality control mechanisms and crisis management at home and in their daily life. Thus, would it be inappropriate to treat them as empowered future managers with about twenty years of dormant or unconscious management learning? Proactively questioning, exploring the causes and estimating the consequences to enhance one's understanding of the happenings around them.

Supported with examples of not so well academically qualified but highly successful business players in the competitive global business arena, it is often said that management is just a judicious application of common sense. And common sense includes being proactively aware, observant and cognizant of the happenings around oneself.

Keeping in view the above and a business environment of unprecedented disruptions, we suggest the following approach and pedagogy for nurturing the spirit of proactive learning and entrepreneurship for the future business players. It would also initiate a life long proactive learning process.

Eaklavya Framework of Proactive Self-learning

One of the ways to teach swimming is to push the learners in the water and let the natural survival instincts come into action. Letting the future swimmers discover the swimmer in them. The same approach may be adopted for aspiring future managers. Why not let the future managers learn about themselves and the nuances of business processes, policies, entrepreneurial pluck and the players in the real business arena. Why not give them a chance to empower themselves? Why not let them experience the process of knowledge based self-empowerment process? Why rote-teach when they would be expected to have a proactive attitude in real business situations? After all, as stated above, they would have been managing their affairs for the past twenty years or more.

If Eaklavya could proactively learn to be the best archer of his time, expecting future business warriors to learn the nuances of business operations based on their own instincts and learning abilities may not be unreasonable, especially in this age of Internet and global learning support systems. After all management is as much a game of heart, guts, intuition, instincts, introspection and proactive learning as it is a game of brainpower, strategic mindset, systematic data analysis, quantitative equations and networking.

To shake out the future managers from their habit of being spoon-fed by teachers and textbooks and to activate the spirit of Eaklavya — proactive self-learning, B-schools may initiate the proactive learning process by providing some relevant questions, if needed. Preferably, the students may be left alone to initiate their questioning process. Let the students define and initiate their learning from their self-defined zero-base.

All learning starts with questions — simple, creative, experimental, or innovative questions. Besides getting a feel of the business dynamics, students would also experience and proactively learn about the complexity of business operations around them. Get a feel and some insights of the various business processes, customer thinking and behaviour. To think out of the box, business school students would have to step out of their B-school box — the classroom. The students should get into the habit of being comfortable with uncomfortable questions; learning to challenge themselves to ever greater proactive learning, in the process discovering themselves and the world around them. Asking questions, defining and solving problems is an integral part of management process.

Given the advantages of information, technology-led information and knowledge era, we feel there is a need to redefine the role of classrooms, blackboards, chalks, teachers, textbooks and even libraries. We need to differentiate between the tools as well as hard and soft skills needed by the future managers and their understanding of different management processes. Teachers need to resist the temptation to teach and allow the learning process to evolve. Let the students feel the need for the skills they need. Learning can be shaped into an interesting experience; but, to be effective, the onus of learning should be on the students.

Thinking of business as a management game and designing a framework for developing a proactive-learning attitude as well as an independent spirit of enquiry in students would be a proactive learning challenge for the faculty as well. In the process B-schools would also acquire and accumulate their intellectual capital.

Initiating the Self-learning Process — Phased Approach

On joining the B-school, the future business managers should be encouraged to do some selected readings and select for themselves an area of business process or social activity as a learning entry point. Or, as an alternative they may be handed over an assignment to examine a specified local business or social issue — perhaps just business news clippings from a local newspaper. In the initial stages the business issue should have local relevance and require students to interact with the local business units. Local relevance is critical to initiate real business learning. The overall learning process may be seen as a proactive learning process through currently live, raw and undefined business or social activity. As far as possible, students should be given full freedom in selecting, profiling and analysing the activity and suggesting ways to improve business or organisation operations in the given context.

Here we would like to suggest that B-schools should try to see themselves as management schools or M-schools. Additionally, making use of the information technology options, think of themselves as mobile M-schools or M2-schools. Also, as management processes are used in every social, commercial and political activity, the management learning perspectives should be comprehensive and inclusive.

We also feel there is no need for any pre-determined rigorous entrance standard for our proposed management schools. The proposed learning system is inclusive, individualistic progressive and flexible. It must be individualised to adjust with the questioning-learning abilities of individual students. It must encourage intellectual curiosity as well as love for detail. Asking questions and self-evaluation are the pedagogic gears of the proposed learning process. We strongly feel that there is an inherent need for individualised intellectual space.

With a proactive learning approach the students can be given the option to learn management in the language of their choice. The process of learning in one's own language and the area of one's choice and would help in energising the vast entrepreneurial and intellectual reservoir in the rural areas. It would help translate the often-heard rhetoric on inclusiveness into reality.

Almost all business is local. Learning local rules and processes of the business game by being part of it would be useful. We feel a rigid learning system tends to create mutual hatred between the learner and the learning system as it restricts self-actualisation of the learner. Today, the information and communication technology provides many creative options for customisation of educational services.

To encourage students to analyse the problems from more than one perspective, they should be given a flexible time frame with full freedom to define, understand as well as analyse the problem in their own way and present at least two alternate solutions for each encountered problem. They should be given all opportunities to make mistakes and become aware of the real happenings in the business arena where they would later have to prove their worth. Let them be as innovative and creative as they can be in analysing the business or social process and presenting their findings with their logical reasoning. The learning experience should be made as restraint free as possible. No question should be considered absurd or irrelevant unless reasoned so by the student asking the question; an alternative to the prevailing per-hour, structured classroom rote teaching. The objective being to let the students proactively observe, experience and gain insights of the why and how of business processes. In the process, also discover the manager in them.

Question-based learning is the basic premise of our proposed paradigm. M-school faculty will only provide help in generating appropriate and innovative questions pertaining to different facets of business such as marketing, finance, use of technology, human resource management, critical success factors and a strategic outlook. Imparting appropriate business language — concepts, terminologies, jargons or vocabulary. If required, M-schools should be able to provide learning support and co-operation from local business units, if the students fail to get it from their own initiative.

Given the paucity of faculty with business experience, the students must be required to present their findings to the full group of students and a panel of faculty members from different disciplines. It may prove to be a valuable new learning experience for all.

In the first phase, the role of faculty should preferably include:

- Developing a creative question-based curriculum of management learning. Active listening and only questioning the students to generate and reinforce intellectual curiosity in them to gain further insights of business operations. Giving them freedom to question, think, analyse and understand the world of business around them as well as the social, cultural and political context in which it operates. It should be inclusive learning. A holistic view of the business operation.

- Keeping in view difficulties in changing thought routines the students be given sufficient time, emotional space, situations, questions to grow and explore their individual growth potential as well as discover their own mental, emotional, physical stamina to learn. Discover their learning avenues and distinct individuality. Assess their strengths and weaknesses. Experience their unique management and leadership styles. Visualise their career paths.

- The grading of students needed for administrative purposes should be dependent on the extent of learning from base level of students and not on any pre-determined fixed scale. The faculty should aim to provide a foundation for learning. A quest to understand the business processes; their dynamics and interface with change. Graduating from the management school should be seen as a work-in-progress for continuous learning in the business arena. They should be ready to walk, trot and gallop with change.

- Business is also a competitive game of mind, body and soul. It would be advantageous to think of team games as an integral part of B-school learning curricula. Individual projects, as they progress, may be creatively morphed into team projects and again re-structured into individual projects, if required. In the process students would learn the usefulness as well as the art and skill of strategic alliances.
- To transform the student research efforts into holistic learning experiences, for students as well as for faculty, feedback in the form of questions for further research in different areas of business concepts and activities such as competition, competitiveness, competitors and also marketing, human resource issues, finance, relevant social issues, use of technology, organisational behaviour should be initiated.
- Even if the faculty wants to see this as a 'live or raw case study' or 'experimental' learning method, they must ensure that students are part of the activity they are analysing; their insights of the business processes under investigation come from 'inside'. Just as a swimmer is part of the water or a player a part of the team, they too must learn by 'experiencing' change, management and leadership processes.
- While students should be made to justify their findings or conclusions, as far as possible, faculty members and other panel members should be restrained from expressing their views in the initial stages. Self-criticism and self-evaluation are to be considered as integral parts of this proactive learning-teaching pedagogy. Students' impulsive desire to look backwards, forward or sideways to gain a perspective of the activity under study, should also be considered as a part of their individual learning process.

- Faculty from different disciplines should be available to provide a question-based holistic approach to learning. Faculty role may be perceived as that of a learning facilitator, mentor or a coach. They should provide questions to instigate learning from different perspectives.
- Local contextual management variables should to be taken note of, discussed and incorporated in the learning process. Keeping in mind the intense cultural diversity, management students need to have a feel as well as appreciation of the impact of the cultural environment on the effectiveness of management processes. Management theories need to be examined in the local-cultural context. This will help B-schools in emerging as local business and management consultancy centres.
- No rote lectures are to be given by faculty to the students. Keeping in view the zero-based approach, students from different disciplines should be encouraged to evolve their own perspectives of the business game. Here also, the emphasis should be on question initiated self-learning and exploring the different aspects of business activities.
- Students should be encouraged to select challenges and issues of new growth areas of the knowledge economy such as entertainment, Internet, e-commerce and different sports as the emerging industries. They should proactively use the Internet as a learning support system as well as make use of other relevant global information sources. Mobile and continuous 24x7 learning should be encouraged.
- The panel for the second phase of presentations should consist of experts from relevant industries. Given the topicality of the topic and research, presence of industry expert would enhance learning value for students as well as for faculty. Students should be encouraged to evolve and formulate their own learning agenda within the overall learning framework.

- Moving up the learning curve, the integrated multidisciplinary proactive learning approach would continue in different semesters, thus enhancing learning in scope, depth and complexity. The scope of assignments would keep moving from local, regional, national to global. Also, assignments should become more comprehensive in scope, use of technology, business issues and strategic perceptions, both for rural and urban markets as well as for different products and services.

Each new interaction should move up the learning value chain with enhanced insightful, question-based, student-teacher interactions; a question-based mutual learning experience for all.

Besides other factors, evaluation pertaining to the assignment may be based on the quality and quantity of the questions investigated.

An appropriate curriculum and credit scoring system can be worked out to make it a flexible and individual learning led degree granting programme.

Here we would like to humbly state that the overall idea is not to reinvent the wheel but to protect the thinking process of students being flattened or crushed by the 'rote' movements of the teaching wheel.

The Paradigm Shift

How does this approach differ from the usual prevailing curriculum and pedagogy adopted by B-schools? There are some fundamental shifts:

- **Individualised Zero-based Proactive Learning:** It is a question-based proactive learning process. Unlike the prevailing systems where students are provided with answers, here, besides various other things, students by questioning will discover management through their own observations. They will experience the management process and the operations of the principles of management, marketing and finance as applied in

different situations in competitive business arenas and in creative marketing warfare. Gain a real playground perspective of the business game.
- **Mentor-teachers:** The role of teacher would be to mentor and position the students on the learning path by questions, questions and more questions, and sometimes also, by questioning the questions raised by students. Keeping in view the real business process as a situational learning focus, the students should be encouraged to engage in lateral and integrative thinking; getting to know the unknown by questioning and exploring. This will help in contextualising theories to situations. Ideally, to awaken the latent knowledge as far as possible, the learning experience for each student should be individualised, uncharted and unstructured to prepare them for an uncertain tomorrow.
- **Question-based Learning:** For every question a student asks, faculty are to provide more questions to instigate holistic learning. As stated above, questioning the questions to give the enquiry appropriate context is an integral part of the proposed pedagogy. Student would not be reading a remote historical case study but experiencing live business situations as an active player in the shifting business scenario. They would explore, analyse and discover the meaning of business and experience change and its day-to-day changing impact. Thus become aware of the competencies needed to survive in a changing competitive business environment. It would make knowledge seeking pleasurable, challenging, contextual and meaningful.
- **Entrepreneurial Managers:** The proposed proactive learning paradigm will help nurture managers with an entrepreneurial spirit and leadership qualities. They will learn to acquire faith in themselves and win trust of others. As they proactively experience dynamics, diversity and complexity of the business world, they will

discover the value of self-management and interpersonal competencies as well as learn to think on their feet. In the process they will discover the leader in them and proactively hone their leadership qualities.
- **Understanding Diversity:** Given our national diversity, with exchange of students and faculty, one would have new evolving local experience and not read the same textbooks or case studies. Perhaps, with time we will develop our regional and local management processes as well as schools of thought or *gharanas* as in music.
- **Rural-management Education:** Nurturing a culture of intellectual curiosity is an integral part of the paradigm. It can easily be adopted to provide management education in rural areas by taking up local, civic as well as commercial activities for understanding their operations and improving their performance. Linking local-rural enterprise with micro and macrofinance would help enhance the vision of local entrepreneurs. Management studies should include local health care and exploring prospects of value addition for traditional crafts and folk entertainment. The vast intellectual energies of the rural masses need to be activated by dynamics of asking and seeking. Students should be encouraged to find markets and create profits out of local skills and crafts. Find creative and innovative ways for generating local wealth by employing local people and using local renewable energy sources, by local enterprise and local entrepreneurs but of global standards for local as well as global markets.
- **Proactive Self-awareness:** The students would become aware of their past encounters with management issues as they would be required to make use of their past management learning in different real-life situations. In the process, students would discover the comparative strengths and weaknesses of the manager within them. Evaluate their capabilities, competencies and the

entrepreneur-manager in them vis-à-vis the prevailing norms in the business arena. Through natural instinct, they would themselves sense the manager, business leader and entrepreneur in them. They would evolve as reality-tested tomorrow-ready business managers. Also, potential business leaders with a clear vision and insight of business operations along with a feel for change and understanding of customers as well as market operations. The leadership learning would also have to be proactively self-customised.

- **Use of modern Global Learning Support Systems:** They would learn to make effective use of the learning opportunities and support systems available to them such as the Internet and experts around them. A real-life situation for managers, giving them the chance to explore and experience their potential. It would generate and reinforce a self-reliant and 'can-do' mindset, leading them to become proactive managers with emotional commitment to wining, excellence and ever-increasing levels of success. They would gain an understanding of the simplicity as well as complexity of business operations.
- **Topicality of Learning:** With the topicality of the problem assigned or selected by them, they would become aware of the prevailing nature of the business environment as well as get a feel of the change and shifting trends in the business landscape. They would acquire pragmatic and intellectual curiosity to feel and experience the change happening around them and also gain an understanding of the nitty-gritty of competition as well as the basis of competitive advantages in the local markets and their cultural nuances. To be effective change agents, they need to feel and experience as well as enjoy the changing challenges of change.
- **Holistic Perceptions:** They will get used to visualising and analysing the business situations from the

perspectives of the total business chessboard. Gain appreciation of the fact that, like individuals, small scale business units as well as large corporations are holistic living organisms, with their own business processes, culture and values. Also, that each situation is different and never repeated. They will also gain a comprehensive perception of business issues as they experience success and failures happening around them.
- **Industry-academia Alliance:** It would form a mutually beneficial strategic alliance between the local industry and academia. An alliance for mutual learning and continuous knowledge sharing. Management being a continuous and constantly changing process would provide new and varied live-learning situations for new and old students at different stages of their learning. There is a felt need to bridge the industry-academia gap.
- **Inclusive:** The questioning-learning centric paradigm is inclusive. The live topicality of the learning effort helps in developing students, faculty, research as well as consultancy activities of M-schools. It will also strengthen the bonds of M-schools with local business community as well as society at large.
- **Time value of Learning:** In real-life situations, business managers and leaders are required to proactively define and demarcate problems and find alternate solutions in the given time frame, in a given situation and with a given objective. As students progress in learning, the selected learning assignments should be made more realistic. Management concerns such as time management, competitiveness, cost-benefit analysis and business intelligence should be incorporated. To make them industry ready, some real-life learning and time-bound frameworks should be provided to students.
- **Modular Structure:** For the benefit of students and for administrative purposes, the M-school degree programme should be made modular — each term-unit

a comprehensive learning experience yet ready to be connected with the next stage. The students should be given the options to pursue the total programme in stages, if they so desire.
- With the above approach, benefits to the students as emerging business players, would include:
    i. Become more observant of the business activities around them.
    ii. Appreciate the value of human relationships in business.
    iii. Learn to learn from their mistakes and failures.
    iv. Acquire a proactive, futuristic and competitive learning attitude.
    v. Become humble, more confident and self-reliant.
    vi. Discover their emotional and intellectual resources as well as the latent leader in them.
    vii. Develop a questioning and improvement-focused learning.
    viii. Enhance awareness of their own strengths and weaknesses in their domain knowledge bases, skill sets and mindsets.
    ix. Broaden their research, creativity and innovation orientation.
    x. Learn to compete individually as well as value adding team players.
    xi. Develop a solution and performance-oriented mindset.
    xii. Understand nuances of critical success factors in a fast-changing business environment prevailing in different industries.
    xiii. An individualised flexible learning time frame.
    xiv. Learn the art of relationship management.

- Students will gain insight of the prevailing business complexities in different industries. Gain understanding of inter and intra-industry relationships.
- With awareness and experience of analysing current business issues from different industries, graduating students will have running starts in industry and also become value-adding members of their corporate teams.
- Students will become aware of the need for their career planning and self-inculcate job-fit traits.
- This will increase the learning efficiency and intellectual capital of business schools.
- India with more than 23 major languages and 22,000 distinct dialects, presents immense opportunities for experiencing cross-cultural issues in business operations.

Given the multivariable dynamics of change in different business segments, students will become aware of the need for perpetual creative thinking, continuous life-long unlearning and relearning as they themselves experience the speed with which ideas need to be transformed into viable propositions or how they become obsolete.

As stated earlier, the above approach is inclusive in the sense that the observations, concerns, learning and research findings of students are simultaneously examined by faculty members from different disciplines and industry representatives. It may also be seen as real-time learning, evaluation and feedback. By continuously probing and asking questions, teachers would help students in their ability to look at one issue from many perspectives. Also, how a particular issue is inter-related with the overall operations of corporations and the society at large.

This paradigm also provides for:
- Individualised proactive learning opportunities, expert learning support systems and framework to gain an in-depth understanding of local managerial and entrepreneurial thinking as well as business operations and business support systems.

- Each student will be able to discover his or her own learning base and build on it. Besides giving them a feel of the prevailing business and social culture, proactive learning explorations would generate confidence in them and provide a chance to discover their own latent creativity and leadership and nurture the spirit of self-reliance.
- While providing for holistic management learning, the paradigm also provides for individualised and self-selected areas of specialisation.
- Given the speed and versatility of information technology enabled services (ITeS), the business education or MBA programmes can be creatively custom designed for individual students with different academic or work experience backgrounds and career plans. Also, e-learning can be flexible, effective and economical. If one can work from home, with appropriate inputs, why not study from home or whenever and wherever one can?
- Mix-match of faculty and industry experts to enhance learning opportunities for students as well as for faculty. Every student will get emotional and intellectual space and time to explore and present his or her ideas.
- Adoption of local 'sick' business units, remote villages or rural areas for study and upgradation in management processes and governance.
- Industry would also gain from new ideas from students, their future customers as well as management resource.
- As they discover their capabilities, students will be able to proactively plan their careers. For guidance and continuous learning, senior students may be appointed as mentors for new entrants.
- Would provide framework and foundation for proactive life-long learning for all participants. Learn the art of sharing knowledge and learning from others.

The above paradigm is expected to create reality-tempered and tomorrow-ready entrepreneurial managers and business leaders.

Way forward

As a way forward, the management schools would be required to do some homework:
- Create their intellectual capital base by acquiring understanding of the nuances of the local business operations.
- As a starting point, schools would need to segment local business from learning perspectives. Identify some tentative learning entry points for students with different academic and work experience base levels.
- Involve local entrepreneurs and business units in the knowledge sharing and mutual learning process. Develop 'learning partnerships' with local, regional and global business organisations.
- Build an appropriate question bank for the use by new faculty. For scaling up operations, alumni and senior students may also be invited in the learning process.
- Evolve innovative and experimental learning processes to develop knowledge bases and business consultancy know-how.
- Create learning teams for each academic discipline to acquire in-depth domain knowledge through relevant question banks to help students in refining, defining and polishing their ideas and proactively positioning themselves in their selected learning environment.

In M-school evaluation, appropriate weightage must be given to:
- The quality and quantity of question banks developed by business schools in different areas of business operations.

- Quality of assignments undertaken by students and their learning. Also, evaluation may be based on the initiatives, diversity, innovativeness and participation involved in the proactive learning processes of students.
- Quality and scope of 'learning-partnerships' developed by M-schools with local business units, NGOs, corporations and other business schools in different parts of the world using information and communication technology options.
- Adoption of local 'sick' business unit or any local, regional, remote village for upgradation in management processes and governance.
- Creative and innovative use of modern learning support systems such as Internet made by students and faculty in creating their intellectual bank.
- Perception of local business units.
- Local business knowledge base and competitiveness improvement programmes for local business units developed by M-schools.

The differentiating factors in the above paradigm include — shift of student mindset from teacher-dependence to question-based proactive learning. Move from textbooks and historical case study based teaching to self-learning by observing real business operations and interactions with active business players. In this paradigm, M-school students are treated as IT savvy managers with over twenty years of 'dormant' management experience. Performance of individual future business managers would be evaluated on the bases of the steepness of their individual learning curve and their perceived potential.

As stated above, to provide holistic learning, M-schools should adopt a 'sick' business unit or a village to improve its managerial effectiveness.

As discussed earlier, the idea is not to reinvent the wheel but to protect the thinking process of students from being flattened, cloned or crushed by the 'rote' movement of the wheel. Also, it will help keep pace with the change. The change engine is embedded in the pedagogy of the proposed zero-based proactive learning paradigm.

When asked to share observations on our above suggested proactive learning paradigm, a senior human resource vice-president of a large MNC said, "Increasingly, business units find themselves operating in a fast-changing environment with often unexpected inflow of disruptive technologies, innovative use of technology and business models, weakening customer loyalties, creative and innovative strategies of global competitors, shifting advantages of global sourcing and outsourcing. To cope with all this and more, business units are looking for managers with a proactive learning attitude and an in-depth understanding of the local business culture. The proactive learning based management learning seems to make a lot of sense to me. In fact I feel it is an intellect-empowering paradigm which would solve many of our problems and provide employment-ready enthusiastic managers." After some discussions on the subject, he concluded with the following remark: "I feel the proposed paradigm will impart holistic, substantive and contextual learning opportunities. Also, B-schools will become value collaborators with industry."

Similarly a senior lady vice-president of a large FMCG-MNC said, "Your proactive learning approach makes a lot of sense to me. Your management education model has a built-in transforming capacity. Learning to be continuous and sustainable learning has to start with a question and needs to be reinforced by questions. I strongly feel it is time for B-schools to critically examine effectiveness of their rote-teaching programme vis-à-vis their objectives, examine strategic options before them and re-align their teaching-learning processes with those of the industry needs. I feel it is time we start with an analytical, open-minded zero-based approach. There is an urgent need to initiate a debate and brainstorming in that direction. Education, also management education, is a lifelong process and not an event. Degrees are just visible milestones. I feel academic degrees should be judged on their ability to initiate further proactive learning and not be seen as an end of the learning process. The suggested paradigm will continuously enrich students and the institutes. It will create a non-stop learning community."

After some discussions, she went on to say, "With the proposed approach, I feel future managers will learn to combine elements of intellectualism and particles of pragmatism. They will be reality dipped. They will also have a clear view of the business process and know-how and an understanding of how and where the money is lost, value is added and profit is generated." She concluded with the following observation: "Shifting from PowerPoint presentations-based information gathered in classrooms to powerful proactive learning in the marketplace would be a major mind-shift for students as well as for B-schools. I wonder how they will react. Both students and the faculty will become learners." As we were about to part she said, "I feel, your proposed look, listen, learn and improve (3L-I) management education paradigm is inclusive and will synergise the e-factors of education, economy, empathy, employability and entrepreneurship. You may also consider naming your proposed approach the 5E proactive management learning paradigm."

"I very much like the zero-based learning paradigm. I would like you to add one more activity in the pedagogy. Each management school should be given the responsibility to revive some local 'sick' or bankrupt business unit. Transform some non-performing assets (NPAs) into performing assets (PAs); not just adopt them for learning as proposed by you," said a retired bank manager.

"With proactive learning by observations, interactions and participation, the students will be able to integrate thoughts, behaviour, emotions and actions. It will provide a holistic, current and futuristic perspective to individuals in selection of their future jobs and occupations as well as in setting their own targets for achievements and performance," said a retired air marshal. After some elaborations he went on to say, "In line with your suggestions, I feel, it would be wonderful if the business school students could adopt a village, a 'sick' business unit, a railway station or a public bus route to improve its managerial performance. These may be taken up as live cases. Also, using video conferencing and e-learning methods one could make it a global learning and knowledge sharing experience. I feel it would also help in increasing entrepreneurial levels. I would like to add that the performance improvements of the adopted units should be evaluated in real business terms; not just talked about or discussed as case studies or for public relation purposes."

After some more discussions, he said, "Having been a swimmer, I like the idea of throwing future swimmers in the water and let them develop the swimmer in them. I feel that is the best way for managers to discover the manager in them. One does not become a sportsman or a game player by watching sports on television or listening to PowerPoint-supported rote lectures in air-conditioned classrooms."

"I feel I am not qualified to make any observations on management education. I did my MBA many years ago from a well-known B-school in USA. Worked for an MNC in various countries for about ten years and since then have been managing my own international trade operations. My knowledge of management education is limited to my MBA days and whatever little readings I have done since then. Like everything else, I feel there are some advantages and some disadvantages associated with the way MBA education is conducted. I would very humbly like to say that the so called management 'theories' such as those of marketing, business strategies or human resource management reinforced by the demarcated right-wrong of management systems as told to us in classrooms tend to limit our thinking options. The real world of business is multifaceted, very dynamic and requires situation-based thinking and decisions. It takes some time to unlearn what is taught in classrooms. It is often embarrassing and also reduces one's standing in the marketplace when one quotes from books or rattles out classroom learnt prescriptions. It is not the fault of B-schools as most of the faculty is not familiar with the ground realities of business. They only teach what they have themselves learnt from teachers who have also not traversed business arenas. I feel your approach would minimise those drawbacks," said an entrepreneur in the electronics industry.

After some discussion on related topics, he went on to say, "As I understand your management education paradigm, it will bring out the latent entrepreneur in the individual students. It will make them more effective managers and insightful enthusiastic entrepreneurs."

"I fully support your suggestions. One big advantage that I see in your proposed system is that gifted students who have special capabilities and needs will be able to learn at their own pace. Extra bright or gifted children often get bored in regular classes. In normal school classes they may often be seen as day dreamers or arrogant. Gifted children usually have adjustment problems. In the proposed system, competing with themselves, they would be able to learn what they want to learn at their own individual pace. Similarly other students will get space to develop their own talent at their own pace," said a university professor of education.

"I have a feedback for you," said the director of a well-known business school. "If you recall, during our previous meeting, a few months back you had mentioned the idea of proactive learning by B-school students. I think, at that time the concept and process was still in a formative stage in your mind. Any way I discussed your idea, as I understood it, with some of our visiting faculty members. Two faculty members, both with doctorate degrees and many years of work experience, were keen to experiment with your approach. During the current term, one is teaching retail management and the other strategic management. After a day of class room teaching, both teachers asked their students to go out in the market and see, observe and report back, in the form of class presentations, their observations on how retailing and strategic management were being actually practiced by business units. Within two weeks there was a big protest by students who were used to the usual textbook-based rote teaching and learning. Their class representatives and a large group of students came to me and said, 'sir, we do not want to be taught like this, by going out and learning on our own. We want to be taught *theories* of retailing and strategic management in class like the other teacher teaches us.' When I asked them to elaborate their thoughts by some example they stated, 'we want to be taught by books and cases as we are taught human resource management — theory X, theory Y and Maslow's theory — so that in our final oral examination and in our job interview we could answer the question, what we learned in human resource management. Similarly we should be able to answer the question, what we learned in retailing and strategic management. We want to learn *theories* and do case studies of good MNCs in class only. We want answers, so we have ready answers for interviews.' Ironically, the subject, Human Resource Management was being taught by a bright faculty member who had never been associated with any business unit. Another teacher friend of mine had a similar experience while trying to introduce the proactive learning pedagogy in his course on strategic management. All that the students were keen to acquire were a few management fads, current jargon and ready-made answers to respond to questions on strategic management during their oral examinations and corporate interviews."

After giving some more interesting details, he said with a smile, "Disconnect between management education and industry is obvious. The disconnect needs to be corrected. Your proposed approach connects B-schools with business needs. I am still in the process of selling the concept of zero-based proactive learning process to students and faculty. Old habits are hard to change. We are all locked in our own thinking processes and past practices in our own comfort zones. Our overall education system is based on rote learning, teaching and evaluation. It is a trade in information and skills, not in creating knowledge. What is passed on and received by students is information and selected skills, not knowledge. As part of the overall education system, the students operate like computer hard disks. They just give back what is given to them. Questioning and original thinking is not encouraged. Analysing problems requires thinking, but our students are in a hurry to have answers. They have no time for questions or understanding the real problems. They want quick and short answers. They are in great hurry to become managers with few impressive 'jargon-commands' — as in an army parade. They want answers, to have the satisfaction of delivering answers during their final verbal examinations and also during the job interviews. What kind of jobs, frankly I do not know."

After further elaborations he went on to say, "I very much like your concept, but there may not be many teachers who will be willing to change or students ready to appreciate the value of proactive learning. By prevailing standards, proactive learning would be uncomfortable learning for students. Shaking students and faculty out of their comfort zones will not be easy. Working with diverse views and ideas is never easy. Flexible systems require more managerial skills. We will have to mobilise and popularise the proactive learning approach. In my own limited way and within the boundaries set by management education regulators I will continue to promote proactive learning."

He concluded with the following statement: "I think we need a vision-based management education process and a dynamic, situation specific performance-based incentive system for B-school faculty. We urgently need to move over from rote teaching to observation and research-based teaching."

"I feel the approach and the pedagogy that you have suggested is urgently needed. There is a big gap between the business realities and the academic world of business education. Wrong business education causes much harm to the business operations." After elaborating on some of the gaps experienced by him, he summed up with an example from his executive career: "Hiring high-profile consultants is a status symbol for some CEOs. While our company was performing much above the industrial average, our CEO decided to hire a globally well-known consultancy firm to enhance our performance. I was abroad on an assignment. When I returned, the consultants were giving final touches to their recommendations. During their final high-profile presentations on their recommendations they presented some very fancy multicolour forms to be filled up by the middle and higher level technical and management personnel of our organisation. The halo effect was conspicuous and the latest business jargons were being liberally used. I was totally confused. To enquire about the objectives of recommendations, I said that while I liked the solution — the beautiful multicolour forms — could I please know the problem that these forms were expected to solve. Frankly I was not being cynical. I was serious in my enquiry. But I was totally taken aback when the consultants failed to identify and define the problem. They had a bagful of fancy pre-fabricated management solutions and were searching for problems. If we had implemented their solution, besides the heavy direct and indirect costs, we would have certainly created some problems for ourselves. All this happened because the assigned consultants had never worked in any industry and had no practical domain knowledge. I feel many corporations must have suffered by following the recommendations from those high-profile consultants." After some elaborations he concluded with the following observation: "Since the practical domain knowledge is built into the suggested learning process, the above mistakes would be minimised. I feel the paradigm will generate insightful managers with appropriate business sense."

"There is a need to take a critical look at management education. The recent scandals in corporate governance, in corporations managed by the managers educated in the best business schools and advised by the best-known management consultants, suggest that there is a need for soul-searching. Corporations have become a critical factor in global development. I personally do not like the word 'administration' in the degree master of business administration (MBA). What we need today is entrepreneurial managers who understand business and can communicate with a soul of business and management. The MBA degree itself needs a soul of management. Perhaps it should be called masters in business management (MBM) or masters in business leadership (MBL)," said the lady director of a large trading house.

"I feel it is a very useful and powerful concept. It is full of common sense. Very simple to understand and implement. It is participative, inclusive and holistic in nature with a built-in new and continuous learning as well as growth orientation. I feel it would have far-reaching effects," said the CEO of a medium size manufacturing unit. After elaborating on his thinking, he concluded with the following statement: "Business schools and other educational institutions will be able to work out their own learning strategies around this concept."

"The critical value that I see for students in the proposed paradigm is that it is based on the foundations of learning to learn and manage one's own learning. The *Eaklavya* approach to learning," said a human resource manager. After some elaborations he said, "There is a fundamental difference between proactive learning and being taught or trained. As I see it, once the proactive learning cycle starts, it would transform our corporate training programmes also. I see a lot of positive value in the proposed proactive learning paradigm. It will also bridge the gap between industry and B-schools." After some elaborations he concluded with a smile, "There is a danger; the proactive learning or questioning may become a habit and make the argumentative Indians more argumentative."

"For me, the apparent value of the proposed management model is the possibility of it being able to produce business leaders. Without the protective cover of meticulous academic research, let me posit that the credibility of leadership is a result of working knowledge and competency to define problems and the courage to follow the path. Appropriate implementation of the proposed model would lay firm foundations of that. Also, leadership needs clarity and courage. This system incorporates both," said a senior talent development consultant.

"I very much like the idea and find it very useful and workable. It will give them a sense of business. It will help students understand and gain insight of the reasons, rational, roots and realties of the business processes. They will have an understanding of the tricks of the trade. I think it will make them forward-looking, solution-oriented and performance-focused managers. My only suggestion would be that each B-school adopting your system should be encouraged to build its own local business and management intellectual capital. Management is nothing, if not creative. It is situational and time specific. It has a limited lifecycle. It has to be original and organic. Each business school has to evolve its own learning curve," said a senior lady executive of a media conglomerate. After some discussions she went on to say, "With all our information technology know-how, why have we failed to develop a virtual university or an effective framework for national learning based on information technology. Proactive learning will encourage the use of global learning sources and create an army of *Eaklavyas*."

After some discussions on her perceptions on the prevailing management education system, she went on to say, "Every business school should also try to create some venture fund for the students. Students should be encouraged to experiment with new business models. All business is local. We need to get an insight into the local business culture."

"I feel there is a lot of take-away value in this paradigm. With the proposed approach to learning, students will get a feel of the real realities of business. They will get a feel of sociology and psychology of work life and role of interpersonal relations with insights into power politics and personality issues at work. They will be able to understand the organisation value chain and job linkages from front line to back offices. And also identify the role of formal and informal groups as well as get an understanding of the dynamics of the various forms of leadership styles and power bases in organisations," said a senior professor of a leading business school. After elaborating on some points he went on to say, "The students will gain an insightful understanding of business processes and will learn to appreciate the real prerequisites to success in the business and corporate world."

After some discussions he went on to say, "I wonder how the leading business schools will react to proposition. There is too much at stake — personal egos and vested interests. It would be hard to accept the fact that we have been wrong for so long. The proactive learning paradigm suggested by you is simple, yet in effect, it turns the management education system upside down. I think it is an appropriate learning-teaching model for the emerging knowledge era."

"I strongly support your thinking. We do not realise the real damage that is being caused to the real industry by the poorly trained business executives passing out of B-schools and the well-known consultancy organisations who employ them. Consultancy organisations prepare fancy 'research' reports based on findings of the B-school graduates who may have, for all practical purposes, never set foot in a business organisation. We all know that most of the B-school faculty have had little or no industry experience. Even in a business consultancy organisation the new recruits are mentored by seniors who may themselves have little or no industry experience. Your proposed scheme will correct this situation. Students will learn by proactive self-experience and proactive self-observations. They will enter the business world with a clear perception of the business operations and management processes," said an entrepreneur in the printing and packaging industry.

After some discussions, he went on to say, "Frankly I see benefits for business as well as B-schools. With this approach, research, teaching and consultancy will all be creatively aligned in mutually compatible and complimentary ways. It will give the B-schools or M-schools, as you like to call them, strong local business intellectual roots. Also I feel it will be of advantage for B-school faculty who have to struggle to balance their tripartite aspirations and responsibilities. It will certainly add vibrancy to the pedagogy. In business, every management policy to be successful has to be situational and contextual. The paradigm provides for both. The added advantage in the paradigm is that it would provide a built-in growth engine for B-schools."

Finally he concluded with the observation, "The current pedagogy and course contents of most B-schools belong to the bygone era. The current failures of large corporations with thousands of best qualified MBAs points to the fact that our B-schools need to take a zero-based approach. MBAs may be part of the problem. We need to critically examine relevance of our outdated, outmoded and ineffective management teaching methods. We certainly need to change. We need to do things differently and more effectively."

When asked to comment on the proposed paradigm, an expat CEO of a consultancy organisation said, "If handled effectively, it is a very simple, innovative and effective way to develop future managers. But, B-schools would have to get out of their comfortable academic cocoons and walk with the industry on the rough, unpredictable and often harsh business terrain. I am not sure if B-schools would welcome your idea. As I see it, it involves a lot of ground work and change of mindset. Changing the mindset is never easy."

After some discussion he went on to say, "The best thing I like about your paradigm is that it is proactive learning with local focus. I feel it will enhance professional values and spirit of personal accountability in future managers. All business, anywhere in the world, is local. Imported or transplanted solutions often do not work. Another very positive angle to it is that students, when they join the industry, would know what they are getting into. Also, I have a feeling that with your proposed proactive learning system, students will have enthusiasm for further learning about the world of business which is usually lacking in the current B-school graduates."

After elaborating on some of the above points he went on to say, "Another important outcome of your paradigm would be that each business school would become an observing, listening and learning institute as well as an active partner of local business. A strategic learning partnership would evolve over time. Also, each business school will have local ethos and unique learning characteristics. With time, it will give B-schools a natural differentiation as well as a framework to cooperate and learn from each other."

As we shook hands to leave he said, "Management education should not be a search for finding gems among stones, but turning stones into gems. That is what this education process will do. I feel it has a fantastic learning as well as take-away value."

Reacting on similar lines a retired director of a well-known B-school said, "What I like about your paradigm is that it will give a chance to the B-school faculty to learn about the real realities of business as they help their students learn about business operations. The students, faculty and the institute will all be learning in the process. During my long tenure in business education, I always had a feeling that I was living in a world different from the real world of business. I always wondered, about the meaningful learning value of the case study method. I often asked myself, does yesterday prepare me for tomorrow or does it become a handicap in a fast-changing business environment?"

"What I find very useful about your approach is the fact that it would take into account the changing job scenarios. The job market is in a state of flux. The students would get a feel of it as they move around in corporate arenas. There is constant shift in the job offerings by different industries. Technology developments, more so new and more effective applications of IT and ITeS, are constantly changing job profiles. Skills that were relevant yesterday may no longer be required today and the skills that the employers need today may be redundant tomorrow," said a senior executive in the investment banking industry.

After some discussions and elaborations he went on to say, "After completing my MBA degree in USA, I had applied to a leading IT consultancy organisation. As part of the selection procedure, I was to pass a written test. I scored 95% marks. However I was rejected and not even called for further interviews. On my persistent enquiry I was explained that the company had a policy to select candidates from those who scored either above 98% or below 70%. They had jobs for out-of-the-box thinkers or those who could work hard and consistently on not so challenging do-as-told jobs. Why have I told you this instance? It is because I feel the job profiles in corporations may not only be changing internally due to innovative use of technology but also by change in locations, due to job-economics and standardization. Thus, it is critical that the B-school students remain in touch with the fast-changing business realities."

Another visiting professor from a leading business school in USA said, "Frankly I find your thinking very refreshing — simple, relevant, workable, useful as well as cost and time effective. With your scheme of business and management learning, the student and faculty exchange programmes will become very meaningful. Currently, I am teaching an identical subject in three different countries using the same book, same cases and same PowerPoint Presentations. Business education has become very structured. Most students join B-schools just to gain a degree. Faculty is evaluated by students; structured teaching, structured evaluation. Innovations and experimentations in teaching get filtered out. Faculty tends to give the students what they want. Old, tested and tried case studies are a nice and easy option for students and faculty. Placements through alumni network in an expanding economy are not difficult. Information and skills are often sold as knowledge. Learning value is fuzzy. It is an easy structured win-win situation for B-schools." After some discussion on the subject he went on to say, "Under your system I would also get to learn and share my learning with others on a continuous basis. It would be a dynamic, live and real situation specific mutual learning experience by information, skills and knowledge sharing by different people with different perspectives. Further value would be added by involvement of the actual game players also."

After sharing some of his experiences in different B-schools in different parts of the world, he went on to say, "It would require extensive groundwork and a sensitive transformational process would need to be worked out. Each business school will have to evolve its own system and local-global strategic learning alliance. I will keenly look forward to your formally formulated framework and see it in action. I will also try it and give you some feedback on it."

He concluded with the following observation: "Education is supposed to take us forward. Education is not inventing the wheel all over again. Effective education should make students sensitive to their surroundings and in looking for things they wish to do differently; searching their own solutions in their own unique ways."

Keeping in view the globally available learning support systems and knowledge era imperative, we feel that the suggested paradigm should not be seen as a negation of the prevailing system but an effort to enhance its effectiveness. It may be seen as a dynamic individualised and flexible proactive-learner-centric or proactive-future-manager-centric continuous learning approach. A system that will generate analytical, creative and intuitive thinking, and provide for broad and general business capabilities and competencies that may be applied to a wide range of jobs in the business and social institutions.

We feel an alternate approach to our above proposed paradigm may be to consider creation of industry-focused M-schools or universities. It may be advantageous to promote competition in generating new ideas to two or more universities for each major industry. Some dedicated to technical aspects while the others to commercial and management. To implement the participative learning concept, the funding for industry universities should come from direct levies from the corporate industry members. It may also be seen as a backward linkage of industry with their talent sources.

While giving a discernable shape to the above paradigm, a question that often came up for discussion was, when and how should management education be introduced in the overall education system? Keeping in view the fast-changing information empowerment of school going children and the need for general awareness of management thinking, we would like to share our thinking on the subject with our readers.

9

Developing Young Intuitive Managers

Sustainable economic and social development of a nation depends mainly on the quality of education, mental growth and attitude of its youth. Also, it may not be wrong to say that today the youth constitute an effective part of a nation's mind, body and soul.

Given a large population and limited resources, imperatives of resource management for us cannot be overstated. Every citizen has a role and responsibility to ensure that national resources are used judiciously and effectively.

Effective resource management may also be viewed as minimising wastage of resources. Resource management is of vital concern to us all — those living in rural as well as in urban areas. For optimal and effective use, we need to understand and appreciate the difference between the renewable and non-renewable resources. Also, we need to appreciate, how the use and reuse of various resources impacts our environment around us; environment that affects our social harmony, emotional sense of well being and also physical health.

As we interacted with people from different parts of the world and from various walks of life, the questions that kept cropping up in our minds were — if baby birds and baby animals can manage their lives and their surroundings, why can't human babies be taught to be young managers. Can we make our beautiful little human caterpillars into more beautiful butterflies that can help make our world a better managed world? Can we empower our children by providing an appreciation of management processes and concepts? Can we develop beautiful little managers who can appreciate the value of the limited resources available to us all? Can they understand the basic principles of management as they observe and practice them in their daily lives? Can we generate a sense of value and confidence in them by making them aware of the imperatives and importance of saving the limited non-renewable resources around them? Can we educate them on how to minimise wastage? Can we create little managers who appreciate and understand the value as well as economics of cleanliness, hygiene and health care?

Conservation of energy and resources has to become a way of life. There is no shortage of problems — big or small. We all need to have problem defining and solution-oriented managerial mindsets. We all need to manage our own little world or area around us more effectively. A little better management will go a long way, if we all do our own day-to-day tasks a little better.

As we discussed the above among ourselves and structured our thinking and earlier chapters, we felt convinced that the world would be a better place if the little toddlers were made more aware of the managerial activities around them. Perhaps we should think of them as beautiful little intuitive managers — future global citizen managers with beautiful minds and compassionate souls.

Besides the business executives, we discussed our perceptions with individuals in the education industry and more particularly with those in primary education.

To keep a focus on the subject of management as a starting point, we decided to define management as an activity or a process that aims to optimise the use of available resources for a given output or objective. The idea was to make the primary school students aware of the different forms of wastages happening around them — at home, in school, in their neighbourhood and in general public places.

"Why not?" said a primary school lady principal. "Yes it is possible to teach management to primary school students. Give them the opportunity to experience nature and management processes around them. In fact, management as you have defined it is already being taught to students in almost every class. A simple definition makes it a very effective teaching tool. Concepts of efficiency and waste minimisation can be explained by interesting stories. Time is a resource. Students learn to manage time at a very early stage. Our activities are governed by time."

After some discussion on the subject she went on to add, "Perhaps, what we need to do is to impart it as a management subject. We need some zero-based thinking. By that I mean, we should try making students aware of the concept of time as a resource and make them sensitive to the use or consumption of time. Then link it up with wastage of different resources happening all around us. All this can be done in a creative and playful way for students and by the students themselves."

After some further discussion she said, "You have presented a very interesting idea; I would like to discuss it with my teachers and also with some enlightened parents and see how we can introduce the concept. At least experiment a little. We can creatively use games, plays, cartoons and group activities to make them our little managers."

As we were about to close our meeting she remarked, "Thinking of our little toddlers as naughty and energetic little managers sounds very enlivening. I feel management should be taught as a creative art. In a way I have begun to think of management as the most creative of the creative arts. Also, I feel this is the most appropriate stage in life to ignite the intellectual fire as well as make them environment-aware citizens."

"If I am not wrong, the word education itself comes from the word *educere*, which means to bring out what is already in and not blindly stuffed in. Thus, for proper education we need to bring out the natural management instinct in our children. The primary purpose of a school should be to guide a child's discovery of himself and his world and to identify and nurture the child's talent. Just as each seed contains a future tree, each child is born with infinite potential. A good teacher is a gardener who tries to bring out the potential already present in the child," said a retired teacher.

After some discussion on the topic she continued, "Management is a normal and natural animal instinct. Like birds and animals and us human beings, we all are born managers. Thus, it would be advantageous to teach management at the primary school level. It would help discover the manager, the leader and other creative talents in the students. It will also help them plan their own career and life systematically. Management, as I see it, is a creative and intuitive social art."

As we were about to leave she said, "The students will not have to be employed to be managers. They will be natural 24x7 grass-roots managers. I wonder how their parents will react to their little charming managers. We are in need of managers, managers and more managers. We need good management in every area of our social activity."

"As I observe the increasing level of intelligence and enthusiasm of small children, I feel there is need to reconsider our approach to developing their intellect in a way that they become more aware of the happenings around them. We need to encourage them to explore and question activities around them," said a senior vice-president in the auto industry.

After some elaboration he went on to say, "The education they get currently, I feel, does not relate them to the happenings around them. It is really surprising that our children do not even know the names or nature of the flora and fauna around them. I feel we need to make them aware of the useful as well as beautiful things around them as well as the wastage and mismanagement happening around them. I am sure that teaching them management concepts and making them aware of happenings around them would make them more observant students, responsible citizens and more effective business leaders as they grow up. I am really very happy that you are thinking on these lines. Also, I do not see any reason why management as a subject cannot be taught to students at the primary level in a creative and interesting way. As they study management they could also act as joyful little consultants to their family members. In helping their families optimise on their electricity, gas and water consumption and minimise wastage of other items. I also see it as an initial stage in the process of creating a value-observing and later a value-generating mindset."

"It would be wonderful if we can impart values and awareness of good management to our children. It would improve the individual software as well as hardware of our society. Our social, economic and political system will become more efficient and effective. But can concepts and principles of management be really imbibed at the primary school level? This you will have to ask the school teachers," said a senior advocate of a high court.

"As you have explained management to me, I feel, we are all born instinctive managers. I strongly feel that management education should be made an integral part of the primary education curriculum. However, it should be done in a creative and innovative way; it should be fun-learning and not an overbearingly imposed learning," said a senior lady teacher of a public school.

Developing Young Intuitive Managers

After some elaborations she went on to say, "The teaching pedagogy should be based on proactive school observation, learning management in a natural way. The students should be encouraged to become proactive and intuitive learning managers. Observe and analyse the good and bad management processes around them. Feel and understand the waste in wastage or why waste is wastage. Management concepts would help them manage their own life more effectively as they grow up."

After further elaboration of her thoughts, she went on to say, "Frankly I think it is a very good idea and would help us develop our children into responsible future citizens. They would develop into more involved, more empowered and I feel more value-adding citizens as well as more responsible social or political leaders also."

"Frankly, although my first response to your proposition was an emphatic no, now having discussed the concept in some detail I see lots of merit and value in your suggestion. I can visualise many useful outcomes in the long-run. Besides various other assignments, having been an industry executive, a corporate human resource developer and an academic teacher, I feel, implementation of such a concept would improve efficiency of various social activities. We see all kinds of wastage around us and all of us need to be aware of it. Another aspect that I like is that the management concepts be taught in the mother tongue of the child and in their own local context, by their own proactive observations at home and around them. Once this is done, they will become proactive managers for life and also have relatively less difficulty in selecting an appropriate career for themselves. This is one of the shortcomings of the current system. Today, it is not uncommon to find even graduates of the B-schools who are not sure of the kind of job they are looking for, for themselves."

After some discussion on his personal work experiences in different industries, he went on to say, "Just like some countries have the requirement of compulsory training in the armed forces to develop each citizen as a potential soldier, the introduction of this concept will make every citizen a manager. No doubt, many of them will grow up to become more effective business, social and political leaders. It will certainly help in developing common sense and gut feel about the management game. Management is an integral part of all human activities."

After some discussion on the education policies he went on to say, "Starting at the primary education level, proactive management learning, based on proactive observations, analysis and open discussions should continue to be a core subject in all academic streams. I feel it will improve the effective use of our scarce resources and introduce the much needed elements of performance and competition in our culture. It will develop caring and creative leaders for different social activities."

After some more elaborations he went on to say, "As a nation we have the responsibility to one-sixth of mankind. We have vast development needs in various areas. And our resources are very limited. We need management competencies in so many different areas, be it in the corporate, public or private rural or urban ventures. Even in the police force, social services, judiciary and the bureaucracy. We need to follow this idea to develop proactive and instinctive managers with a focus on performance and wastage minimisation."

"To nurture little toddlers as proactive, naughty, exploring and investigative self-aware managers is a wonderful idea. It would be a good learning experience for teachers as well as parents also. Especially as it would be contextual it will be more meaningful. After all effective and waste-free management is needed in every aspect of personal and social life," said a senior IAS officer who had served in the Ministry of Human Resources for a few years.

After some discussion he went on to say, "Frankly, I feel we need to use our own education methods also; make good use of our *Panchatantra* stories to teach management. After all, our kings were trained to become good managers by such live examples, based on nature and happenings around them, so why not adopt them even today. To get the best out of our resources we need proactive managers." He concluded with the following observation: "We need a cadre of Common Man Managers (CMMs)."

"I think it is a wonderful idea. Let me explain to you from my own experience. During my MBA programme, one of our teachers often repeated the phrase: 'speak Management not English.' It took us a while to understand its significance. What he meant was, we were required to speak in terms of measurable, meaningful, relevant and objective or target-focused factors. He also demonstrated that management is creative but has to be meaningful in measurable terms. Our young ones will learn to speak management in a natural way what took us a while to learn in business school. I full heartedly support your approach and see great intrinsic value in it," said a senior business executive. After some discussion he went on to say, "We often lose lots of time because of semantic differences, like the parable of the six blind men and the elephant. I feel this will help us define and see the management issues more clearly and comprehensively."

"The way we educate our children would determine the path that our economy and society is likely to take. The curriculum followed in schools is fundamental in shaping the future. A school through its teaching methods can help children discover and develop their intelligence and potential, their creativity, or stem their learning initiative. I feel teaching of formal management principles and policies at the school level in a creative way would transform our national ethos and bring about a solution-oriented approach in our future generations. It will create an inclusive society.

Little useful suggestions, in the long-run can save a lot and also result in lots of extra benefits. I see it as a transformational approach to education," said the senior lady principal of a school located in a rural area.

"I do not know much about management education and how it is taught, but if management can be taught to our little kids, as you have explained, then I feel it would be very good for us all. It may change our thinking. Children are curious. It is easier to explain things to children because they have open minds and are eager to learn. They are more enthusiastic about learning. They will learn fast about the problems faced by us. As they grow up they will be able to understand the problems faced by us in the rural areas. They will be able to help us in finding appropriate situation-specific solutions to our problems in areas such as agriculture, ecology and water management. We senior people would also like to attend management classes," said a village *panchayat* chief.

"I wholeheartedly agree with your proposition. To transform our country and get the best out of our people and resources, we need management-empowered citizens. It would give our country sustainable competitiveness in the global business arena," said a retired major general associated with education.

After sharing some of his experiences with us he went on to say, "The most critical building block for building a country is education. But education has to be appropriate and relevant. The competitiveness of a country depends on the productivity of its workers. The productivity of workers depends on the quality of education. Introduction of management thinking at the initial stages of the education process would go a long way in improving the efficiency of our social and economic institutions. I feel, little smiling, proactive, observing citizens with a managerial bent of mind will be participative and empathetic solution providers and not cynical citizens. Management education would also help in creating emotionally self-reliant and proactive career-developing and skill-learning citizens."

As we were about to leave he said with a warm handshake, "Yes, we surly need solution-oriented management-empowered little soldiers. What I like most about this approach is that students will slowly grow up with appreciation of management happenings around them. They will have time and freedom to appreciate the game, mystery, music, dance and drama of management in action. They will get a good feel of the mindset, heart and soul of management, and business operations around them. I wish you all the luck. We need lots of good management around us."

"According to me, management is all about doing things in a systematic manner to achieve some pre-determined purpose. I feel children should be taught effective management skills in their primary schools so that they grow up to be effective citizens who contribute to the progress of society and country in a more concerned, committed and productive manner. Also, I feel management can be taught in a very creative and interesting way using very interesting games, stories, group activities and little project assignments where the whole family as well as the community may also be involved," said a senior school teacher.

"Oh there is so much to be learned from nature. One can learn a lot by observing the behaviour of birds, animals and even plants around us. Teaching children to observe nature and then creatively introducing concepts of different aspects of management to them is a wonderful idea. One can even learn about competition, strategic management and various other aspects of management, just by observing, analysing and discussing with classmates," said the lady principal of a primary school.

After elaborating on some points she went on to say, "Teaching management at the primary school level and in regional languages would be a very interesting challenge.

Many of the management concepts would need to be adapted to local requirements. I have often wondered whether we have appropriate words in our regional languages for concepts such as competition, value-addition, value-chains and creative destruction. It will also enrich our regional languages."

After some discussion on the primary education process, she concluded by saying, "It is a very novel idea. The definition and the concept you have provided is very effective as well as comprehensive. It will be a nice learning experience for us all. I will discuss with my teachers and we would certainly explore its adaptation within our prevailing curriculum. I strongly feel concepts such as waste management, kaizen, opportunity-cost, time management, marketing, ABC analysis, objective-based management and some leadership concepts can easily be introduced in some very simple and creative ways. Information technology and games can be effectively used as teaching tools."

"It is a very interesting concept. Like birds and animals around us, we are all born managers. Thus, let's not wait for an MBA to gain insight into the management process or learn the soft skills of managers, but rather incorporate each one of them in our daily life right from the primary school level. To be effective and useful it has to have an inclusive approach. The teaching process must involve proactive teachers, proactive parents and a proactive school management as well as society. The proactive learning game must be proactively played by all participants. In rural India, *panchayats* should also be involved in the management teaching-learning process," said a senior primary school teacher.

"Frankly my first impulsive reaction was a no. Your idea or suggestion sounded almost ridiculous; sorry for the language and for being rude, but on second thoughts it does make sense to me and frankly now I feel, why not," said the senior lady principal of a well-known primary school.

After some discussion she went on to say, "In some ways we are already doing it but not with the same objective or focus." She summed up with a smile, "I will try and see how we can introduce this line of thinking even at the nursery and early primary level. Maybe we will rename our school as the Tiny-Tots Management School." After a pause she said with a smile, "I hope the IIMs will not see us as their competitors."

"I feel it is a very good concept and valuable social thinking. The health and performance of every social, economic and political activity, function, and process depends on the quality of management. Management is the basic spirit of modern age. I feel management education at the primary level should be a learning-focused process and not any goal-focused process. Students must be given complete freedom and the chance to experience the Zen, yin and yang of management as they move along their learning curves," said a retired lady external affairs officer.

After some discussion she went on to say, "I may sound out of context, but I feel that management education at the primary level would go a long way in transforming some weaker sections of the society into micro-entrepreneurial classes. It would be wonderful if we could provide microfinance to the budding entrepreneurs and creatively create rural, semi-rural and urban centres for small roadside and special-zone entrepreneurs, like the weekly bazaars. Instead of the police chasing them away, they should be encouraged to set up their ventures in specified areas, on specified days and the police should provide protection to them. They should be provided safety, security and management education to nurture their entrepreneurial enthusiasm."

After some elaborations she went on to say, "If some roadside game players can become the cherished boys in blue and national hockey and football players, why can our roadside entrepreneurs not become a part of the India Inc., or competitive national and global business players."

"It may sound a bit too farfetched, but I feel introduction of management education at the primary school level will help in producing managers who can feel management in their veins and can help in developing improved standards in management systems in different industries and at different levels. It will also help in the ongoing 'professionalisation' of management and management consulting. From my experience, I feel most management consultants lack the emotional and intellectual feel for business operations. They are not in touch with the soul of business. Management schools are too skill focused. This proposed system will help develop managers with clear concepts as well as an analytical vision for management processes," said the patriarch of a large business family.

After some discussion on the subject he went on to say, "We tried to introduce this system in the family but have failed. The children go to business units mostly for fun and enjoyment than for learning. Our staffs also pamper them. But I feel if the children visit business units as students and ask questions and if they are also asked questions in school about their visits, they will become more observant and also better business researchers in future. They will also become more proactive learners or *Eaklavays*, as they observe business operations and management processes all around them — at home and in marketplaces. The process will nurture the child's innate curiosity. "

After sharing experiences of his efforts to train family members to become future entrepreneurs, he went on to say, "I feel today children can be taught management by many innovative and creative ways such as video games, school functions, arranging periodical school bazaars, animation of our old *Panchatantra* stories and creative business and management games in classrooms. Teachers should be given a free hand in evolving their teaching methods within their local context — in urban as well as rural areas. I feel it should be learning by exploration, observations and analysis only."

After some further elaborations, he concluded with the statement, "I feel this education approach will create empowered, courageous, conscientious, creative and caring citizens; citizens who understand the nuances of social, economic and political processes and ecological issues."

"The prevailing democratic and capitalistic practices are not the most desirable or efficient political and economic systems but are the best out of the bad choices before us. Even that is debatable, as we see the trends in many countries. Capitalism, as we know, is based on the principle of self-interest. Social cynicisms are natural. However, from our national perspective, we need to develop institutions that strengthen these systems to serve us more effectively. I think that your proposed system would help us in that direction. It will provide future citizens with a knowledge base to define problems more clearly, skills to solve problems more effectively, and solution-oriented proactive mindsets to be solution-focused citizens. Frankly, I like it very much and feel it would be a step in the right direction," said a senior retired police officer.

After some discussion on the topic he went on to say, "Our current economic system is based on the assertion that private vices and self interest become public benefits. It needs to be accepted with insightful understanding. I feel children would become more appreciative citizens once they have experienced its ethos. They will grow up to be responsible managers with understanding and insights of our prevailing systems."

"What they teach or do not teach at Harvard or IIMs I do not know, but I feel management can be taught and effectively taught in primary or junior schools. We need to re-define management and management education. We can effectively create our little management schools. I also believe that we all are born managers. We need to be made aware of our latent inborn managerial talents," said the senior lady principal of a nursery school.

After some discussion she said, "I feel, it is more difficult to inculcate leadership qualities at the college level. Leadership is an internal process. It has to be instigated, provoked, and challenged early in life. Leadership learning is not for grown-ups. It is for soft and tender hearts. I strongly feel that the school is the right place to start the process for developing a socially aware and committed leadership. For developing the Chandragupta in them, we need to play the role of Chanakya."

After some further elaborations she concluded with the statement, "By letting children explore, question and assimilate from their surroundings, we will be helping them develop their own individual identity. They would develop into creative leaders and not a mere imitative or derivative."

By and large the reactions of the people we contacted in the industry were very positive. Some suggested that the idea should be floated and discussed in public and expert forums, but its adaptation and implementation should be left with the schools. To be effective, an idea of proactive learning should be proactively adopted. Media and society have a very important role to play to make it a shared learning experience.

The vision of beautiful little managers, taking little steps to change their surroundings for the better was enthusiastically received by most of the people we interacted with.

Continuing with our questioning and learning process we tried to assimilate an overview of the future challenges.

10

Future Challenges and a Way Forward

Appropriate education forms the backbone of a society and is one of the most important indicators of a country's real growth and development. Also, the rise and spread of a knowledge economy at the global level has reinforced education as the key economic and business driver. Knowledge era will require a new set of knowledge bases, skill sets and mindsets. More than just the education level, as normally understood in relation to the level of degree, it is the attitude or mindset to self-learn, unlearn and relearn that is the critical factor. Future business leaders will have to be proactive learners.

The imperatives of proactive learning, unlearning and relearning are reinforced by the accelerated pace of disruptive technology in the business arena along with the unprecedented convergence and divergence of industries. These changes impact the structures, job profiles as well as the strategic thinking of corporations. The proposed paradigm provides a framework for a holistic as well as a situation-specific learning paradigm that minimises waste due to unrelated learning. Mobile and immediate global connectivity, along with the increasingly vast reservoir of information made instantly available by the Internet, provide a versatile learning support system. Thus, the need for learning the art of question-oriented learning.

Whatever our perceptions of the future, it will be a world of unprecedented changes and challenges in every area of human endeavour. It will be a different world — an uncharted world of the knowledge era. It will require new leadership mindsets. It will call for management, more insightful management, more innovative and creative management, for management of talent, technology, institutions as well as processes in every social, economic, and political endeavour. A proactive learning attitude would be a critical success factor.

Keeping in view the global perspectives of limited resources and rising aspirations of people, the management education community needs to critically examine its role and responsibilities. We need to objectively examine our opportunities as well as challenges and carefully work out our roadmaps to the future. Perhaps it is time for a zero-based approach. The proposed paradigm may be a way forward in that direction.

Given the instant global connectivity, business players will have to learn to manage local, regional and global issues amicably. There is a felt need to shift from government and a destiny-dependent way of life and culture to a proactive, self-determined, destination-oriented mindset. To take advantage of the evolving opportunities and to be competitive and grow in the fast-changing environment, individuals will have to proactively empower themselves with required information, knowledge and managerial skills. Proactively develop new capabilities and competencies. For an uncharted tomorrow we need an unscripted management education; managers who have a feel for change. The basic challenge is to understand the nature, intensity and direction of change.

Business players as well as corporate team leaders have to critically analyse and evaluate the tacit and implicit shifts from the industrial era to knowledge era. Opportunities and imperatives of the fast-evolving knowledge era need to be decisively comprehended. The proposed paradigm prepares managers for that kind of future.

Trying to manage the knowledge era challenges and opportunities with industrial and agriculture era mindsets would create more pain rather than profits for business players as well as organisations.

Globalisation is a sum total of local realities. Global corporations are a sum total of their local operations. For sustainable growth, global corporations need to be flexible in their operations, open to new learning and willing to draw in creative energies from all their local sources. Global organisations need leaders who have local insights and global perspectives; leadership that nurtures proactive learning and ideas. The paradigm initiates a proactive learning process and provides foundations for optimal future growth.

Notwithstanding the availability of various sophisticated analytical tools, management decisions and actions are often intuitive, situation-specific, common sense and common purpose processes. Economic sustainability and social development of a society would largely depend on the physical, mental and emotional growth as well as attitude of its youth. Given the increasing speed of change, future generations of managers and business leaders would have to be proactive in being aware of the real challenges and opportunities before them. They need to be information and talent empowered for the fast-evolving knowledge era.

As more and more organisations, small, large and global, realise the business imperatives of inclusive growth in the communities they operate in, advantages of proactive learning and the need for redefining business models will become apparent. To be effective, creativity and innovations would have to be locally contextual. Gaining a local insight is an integral part of the proposed paradigm.

Also, the imperatives of proactive learning should not be overlooked as we march towards a knowledge-based economy. We need to critically examine our assumptions towards education, learning and economic activities or work. There is a felt need for a mutually beneficial coalition between education and industry. Appropriate talent development and talent needs are two sides of the same coin.

Industry needs managers who can analyse as well as intuitively feel the nature and direction of change. Together, we have the capability to write and build our future. We have the technology support learning options. We need the moral and emotional courage to do it. Our social, cultural, economic and political institutions need effective managers with insights of management processes. We also need innovators, entrepreneurs and leaders with local insights. The management development initiative presented in the earlier chapters is an effort in that direction.

We realise that resistance to change is natural. We are driven by our fundamental human impulse to preserve what we have and are comfortable with. We like to rationalise our habits. The proposed learning-focused paradigm recommends teachers to resist the temptation to teach and let the individual future managers and business leaders evolve their own learning process. It is a student-led learning process and teachers are expected to provide learning support in the form of appropriate questions and inquiries. Education to be educational has to be a proactive knowledge acquisition, knowledge creation and a knowledge sharing process.

As the social, cultural and national boundaries are slowly eroding, it would be advantageous for each individual, corporation and nation to take a global perspective. Notwithstanding their origin, individuals and corporations would have to be accountable to the communities in which they operate. The global fabric is woven with local strands. The growth and sustainability of transnational business operations will depend on their local understanding and acceptance. International corporate bottom lines would need to reflect local participation, enhancement of local economic vitality, support for environmental health and improvement of social integrity.

As more and more corporations and also some individuals become larger economic entities than many nations, business diplomacy would need to become an integral part of the global business game. Increasingly corporate and individual affairs are becoming social affairs. Accountability, responsibility, fairness and transparency of one's actions would become generally expected norms. Also, with increasing democratisation of market economy, corporations and politicians would have to learn from each other to more effectively serve their constituencies of consumers and voters. As in the case of industry, with enhanced empowerment of individuals in the information era, politicians would have to learn to work collaboratively with their voters. Also, with the increasing use of e-governance, the ruler-ruled concept would have to give way to collaborative partnerships for social development. Corporations would need to become more consumer centric and politicians more voter centric. Local insight would be a critical success factor for each. The proposed zero-based proactive learning framework caters for that.

To meet new challenges of the multifaceted dynamic fast-evolving knowledge era, we have to adopt new ways of learning, working and living. It has to be done by us and ourselves in a proactive way — work in proactively learning teams with synergising leaders longing to know, learn and transcend the thought barriers.

With the growth of mobile and e-commerce, corporations in their own interest would have to adopt more transparent governance norms. Sustainable global operations require global citizenship norms. Organisational behaviour of global corporations would have to be in sync with prevailing local social values and culture. Besides gaining insight into the local business culture, corporations would need to understand and learn to cooperate with different government agencies, NGOs, local business partners and competitors. All this will require continuous proactive learning. The above backdrop and the identified scenario shifts, enhance relevance of the suggested paradigm.

Scenario Shifts

Taking into account the inputs of experts in the earlier chapters and observing some discernible trends in the current scenario, besides various other variables, we feel the future business and social scenario will include:

- **Enhanced Digitised and Empowered individuals:** Increasing number of people in different parts of the world would feel progressively more comfortable with the use of information technology. National and global spread of information technology savvy population would lead to individual empowerment as citizens, consumers, voters and self-actualised career planners. Besides other changes, knowledge era operational realities include Internet, e-commerce, m-banking, e-politics, e-governance, e-learning and e2-citizens (electronically-empowered citizens). Creatively used information systems help in making management and proactive individual learning processes easier, cheaper and more effective. We believe proactive learning and empowerment are interdependent. Also, empowered individuals are likely to have greater social voice, individual identity and a self-determined direction.
- **Localisation-led Globalisation:** For survival and growth, globalisation will need to deepen its local roots; gain insight into the local business practices and consumer behaviour. Besides 'localising' their products and services, corporations will need to attune their corporate communications to local folk music and mores.

Transnational corporations will need to be sensitive to local social, political and cultural landmines. Localisation is an imperative for sustainable globalisation. In their global operations, corporations will often need uniquely local solutions to uniquely local problems. Taking local consumers for granted would be a grave mistake of global managers.

- **Enhanced Entrepreneurial Ethos:** Information and knowledge-empowered individuals of the knowledge era are likely to be proactive individuals who decide their own destinations and create their own roadmaps. Fundamentally, entrepreneurship is about gaining and utilising the process of wealth creation. The suggested pedagogy lets future entrepreneurs proactively acquire an insight into the wealth creation process. As explorers they would perhaps like to set their own learning agenda — see, experience and evaluate realities of challenges as well as opportunities from their own intuitive perspectives. Proactive learning would be their *mantra* to remain competitive.

- **Faster and shorter learning-unlearning-relearning Cycles:** Factors such as innovations and innovative business models, increasing speed of globalisation, disruptive technologies and creative use of disruptive technologies would warrant proactive talent with zest for learning, unlearning and relearning. Competitive advantages would originate from active listening, observing, questioning and faster proactive learning.

- **Facilitating Leaders:** In the knowledge economy of proactive learners, to optimise talent performance, effective leaders would need to facilitate maximum creative inputs from their individual team members. Their major role would be to provide an effective work environment for optimal performance, creativity and commitment. Thus, effective leadership would nurture and coordinate leadership initiatives of individual team members towards corporate goals. In the complex, diverse, multicultural, dynamic global environment, leadership that leads by nurturing proactive learning leaders would provide sustainable competitive advantages.

Keeping in view the above and what has been discussed in earlier chapters, we feel management education and management education communities need to redefine their role. We need to take a zero-based analytical look at the prevailing management education processes and juxtapose our social, economic and political development philosophies along with the available technology support options, for effective education and talent development in an information and knowledge era.

Whatever the system, we feel students should be put through a proactive learning process. The system should be flexible enough to allow individual students to proactively learn at their own pace and in areas of their interests. A synergistic partnership between industry and academia as suggested in our paradigm, we feel, would go a long way in developing talent that is job-fit as well as a proactive team player with a business and social process insight. Given the information technology options and knowledge era imperatives, we need to take a zero-based approach to nurturing talent and leadership traits.

Notwithstanding the global popularity of the MBA degree programmes, keeping in view the often expressed mismatch between corporate needs and output of B-schools, to minimise human resource wastage, we feel there is an urgent need to introduce a proactive learning pedagogy as elaborated in earlier chapters. Human resources are too sensitive and precious to be processed and developed as industrial products with standardised processes. A local situation and job-specific approach would be more cost and human resource effective. We need to think in terms of keeping in view the critical role of appropriate talent in effective management of various social, political, economic and cultural institutions. We need to evolve appropriate talent development processes and effectiveness measurement tools.

We also need to creatively use the available learning-teaching options provided by information and communication technologies. Today, every desktop and laptop computer has the potential to be an effective education and management learning centre. Proactive learners need mentoring more than monitoring; more questions rather than answers.

Executive development programmes, which may be seen as an integral part of management education, should also be seen as experience sharing and mutual learning programmes. Here also, as in the suggested proactive learning pedagogy, faculty would have much to offer and much to learn through their question banks. The programmes can be strategically coupled with research and doctoral as well as post-doctoral programmes of M-schools. Corporate executive development programmes may also be creatively used by M-schools for developing junior B-school faculty.

It may not be wrong to say that the critical success factors for products and services in the global business success include their local-culture specific 7As — awareness, accessibility, availability, affordability, attractiveness, acceptability and amiability of the sales process. The nuances of all these can be proactively learned, in a given context, under the guidance of questioning M-school faculty. The proposed paradigm would help in gaining an insight into the prevailing customer thinking and their decision making processes. Customers are local and constitute the very basis for business.

We feel there is a felt need to use M-school classrooms as learning laboratories, with an innovative and experimental approach; combine rigour and research with relevance and change. We need to engage business executives in the management learning processes to enhance utility and credibility of various management models and theories. In the fast-changing business environment besides a local insight, the 'globality' of managerial mindset is essential.

As suggested in the earlier chapters above, given the uncertain fast-changing business environment and the uncharted future, there is a need to take a zero-based approach. Nurture zero-based management thinking and leadership. Historical trends need to be analysed, modified and managed in the present context. New directions need to be inclusive. Entrepreneurship explorations and business leadership development programmes need to be forward looking and change oriented. Imperatives of disruptive change, inclusive growth and harmonious survival have to be objectively and critically analysed. We need to change the change and make it inclusive.

Keeping in view the current and evolving competitive imperatives, the suggested alternative management education model would develop managers and business leaders who can cope with the frontline strategic thinking needs in the global business arenas.

The global village has many deceptive images. In many social and economic areas, we continue to operate with industrial age assumptions. To avoid the black swan syndrome, we need to understand the prevailing dynamics and face the real realities of linguistic, social and cultural diversities in the domestic and global arena; evaluate the opportunities and challenges offered by the information technology and knowledge era, and use them to our advantage in developing future business players as well as leaders with a local insight and a global mindset.

The future, as we see it, is expected to be full of surprises. As we move into the unknown zone of business environment, we should be geared-up and not be surprised by surprises. We need to be mentally and emotionally prepared. An experimental proactive learning paradigm helps in preparing for the uncertain and unknown environment, full of unexpected surprises. Given the uncertain turbulent times ahead, each business team player would have to be a proactive prime mover — a leader in his or her own way. This is an effort in drafting a roadmap in that direction. Also, it is our humble salute to the spirit of proactive learning.

We feel the management learning process should be an enthusiastic odyssey of discovery. The paradigm suggested will develop managers and business leaders who understand change intuitively and see change as a challenge and are not afraid of it. The suggested proactive learning process will produce curious, smart and confident managers ready to lead in the uncharted business territory. Also, as we see it, there is heavy business weather ahead. We would need cool, calm, collected insightful game changers.

Our Management Books

18 MANAGEMENT COMPETENCIES
Saugata Mitra
A noted Human Resource professional and Analyst and the Chief People Officer with Mother Dairy, New Delhi
Seema Bangia
A HR professional and General Manager, Human Resource with ZTE Telecom, India
Jayati Mitra
Founder & CEO Abbscissa Consulting

With the rapid expansion of global markets, managers in business enterprises are struggling to balance the need to think globally and act locally. The uniqueness of this book lies in its simplicity in defining the basic nature of a competency. This work does not pretend to be the last word on competencies, but it can be useful as an invaluable reference guide, a ready reckoner or a HR handbook for the practitioners at various levels.

2008 • ISBN 978 81 207 3942 6 • 5.75x8.75" • 224 pp • Rs 600

LEADING FROM THE FRONT: From Army to Corporate World
Col S.P. Wahi
Former Chairman, ONGC

This book is a treatise on management by a world-renowned technocrat, a legend with over 58 years of hands-on-experience, within the country and abroad. It is an invaluable guide which covers topics such as leadership development, long-term vision for growth of business, oil security and management of the oil sector for energy security and the impact of emotional intelligence of a leader and his knowledge of human psychology.

2008 • ISBN 81 207 3539 0 • 6.5x9.75"
• 288 pp • Rs 695, £ 29.99, US $ 49.95

BEST BUSINESS PRACTICES FOR GLOBAL COMPETITIVENESS

Dr Prashant Salwan
Chairman of International Business Area and Corporate Relations, IIM, Indore

Based on the information gathered from case studies, fact sheets and a range of self-assessment tools and the author's interaction with academicians, bureaucrats, business executives and industrial experts, this book attempts to bring together the best management practices and provides the readers with a toolkit of practical advice.

2007 • ISBN 81 207 3255 1 • 7x9.75"
• 296 pp • Rs 800, £ 35.99, US $ 59.95

HUMAN RESOURCE MANAGEMENT:
A Contemporary Text
Fifth Revised Edition
Bhaskar Chatterjee

Contents: Evolution and Emergence • HRM and the Business Organisation • Human Resource Planning • Recruitment, Screening and Selection • Training and Development • Job Analysis and Design • Performance Appraisal • The Japanese Approach • Organisation Structure • Organisation Design • Organisational Culture • Leadership • Change Management • Index

2009 • ISBN 81 207 • 7x9.75"

for complete Catalogue visit www.sterlingpublishers.com